"Could I be jealous of the way he was touching my horse? Yep ... I was."

Carly Kade, *In the Reins*

———————————

"If you have it, it is for life. It is a disease for which there is no cure. You will go on riding even after they have to haul you on to a comfortable wise old cob, with feet like inverted buckets and a back like a fireside chair.

Monica Dickens

———————————

"You ask and do not receive, because you ask amiss."

James 4:3

THE BREATH

OF

HORSE CRAZY

The Love Affair Between

Women and Horses

Lynn Baber

Published by Ark Press, USA

ISBN 978-1-938836-28-2

Some of the stories shared may have been combined, with names and minor details changed to preserve the privacy of individuals. I'm deeply grateful to the women who contributed under their own names. Readers can learn more about them at www.LynnBaber.com.

Table of Contents

Introduction

"I slept on that horse, and ate breakfast, lunch and dinner on that toy Wonder pony. When I woke out of a dead sleep I cried, because I wasn't done riding my Wonder horse. From that moment, the breath of horse crazy was instilled in me."

Jessica Shively

Why do you love horses? Husbands, fathers, and sons try to understand us, but often give up, accepting that just as kittens grow up to be cats, the horse-loving woman in his life was born that way. She is a force of nature, unknowable, unchangeable, and the smart ones learn it's better to accept than resist. A duck is a duck, and there's no payoff trying to figure out why a duck isn't a platypus when both have bills and lay eggs. It simply is.

You breathe and you love horses. What's so difficult to understand?

Women love horses because we are in love with love. It's our nature to adore warm fuzzy bodies with enormous liquid eyes, perky ears, and enough hair to practice any plaiting, weaving, or styling technique. Add to that gorgeous image a half ton of sculpted muscle and the sleek elegance of an arched neck with flowing mane. If that weren't justification enough for your equine passion, pile on the hairy Disney-esque characteristics of ponies, God's suggested companion for women and girls tempted by the mystique and challenge of bad boys.

Love is a jewel to women. What lady worth her

breeches has too many jewels? Throughout our lives we collect love; our first love a precious pearl that generates the desire for more. Love comes in many forms, each one adding a pearl of great price[1] to your collection. Horses constantly add pearls, inspiring and offering love in many forms. Whether you presently have a single pearl pendant or triple-wrap pearl bracelet, love is the center of everything. Your collection includes a pearl for every person and critter you've loved.

Women do for those they love. It's in our DNA.

The very thought of horses changes my spirit; inhaling their sweet aroma, feeling my fingers pulling softly through silky tail hair, my heart translating their secret language of snuffles, whuffles, and whinnies. I've been blessed to live with horses for over thirty years, trading in my training facility for a barn shared with my husband, four horses, two dogs, and a cat. Until I was thirty-three years old, I held the dream of horses in my heart, doing everything possible to ride, pet, talk to, or simply be near one. This book is for my horse-crazy sisters, those who are living the dream and those still clinging to hope that one day hers will come true.

Horses are magical, spiritual, frustrating, and graceful teachers and students. They tolerate, resist, endure, forgive, and commit. The love affair between women and horses is real, enduring, and charged with emotion. Life with a horse will bring you to your knees in joy, gratitude, and sorrow when the time of parting comes.

My equine career started late, but as you'll discover from the amazing women who share their stories with you

---

[1] Matthew 13:46

in *The Breath of Horse Crazy*, late doesn't mean never. My success in the business as a breeder, trainer, judge, and consultant was a gift from God for His glory, illustrating both His sense of humor and perfect stewardship of resources; God wastes nothing. The darkest places in my life became places of strength, useful when speaking with women looking for hope. My years as an equine entrepreneur taught me lessons I couldn't learn anywhere else because each one either blessed my heart or broke it.

Horse-crazy isn't a fad. It's true love.

As a geeky horse trainer, the practical part of this book wasn't as difficult to write as the emotional element. My gift is working with horses. Communication with horses is mostly nonverbal, connecting on a spiritual level, riding on waves of energy pulsing with more meaning than all the words in this book put together. Horses know that I get them because they know I care.

I speak horse.

My emotional vocabulary has few words, yet in the company of horses I feel like Elizabeth Barrett Browning. Simple requests and body movement, the energy of intention, proven commitment, peaceful spirit, and putting the horse's welfare before my own make up the vocabulary used to make and keep promises; filling in or sweeping clear as quickly as a horse's thoughts, fears, joys, resistance, submission, offers, withdrawals, and imagination change from hot to cold and from timidity to boldness.

I do whatever's needed to keep the dance balanced, meaningful, and progressive. Nothing is more important than maintaining the connection and keeping my promises. Horses offer because you offer. Horses are the most generous and honest creatures imaginable, treating you precisely as you deserve - unless they show you grace. Unmerited. Inexplicable in its simplicity, flowing from a heart fifteen to twenty times the size of your own.

Horses are also frustrating, resistant, and immovable beasts in the presence of a demanding human. When that happens, you know you screwed up. The horse is honest in his evaluation. When you fail, he lets you know it.

Humility is part of life with horses. Everyone makes mistakes. When you do, learn from them. The horse only wants what's best for everyone because it's his nature. Horses are all about herdship, relationship, and connection. What's not to love about that?

I can't telepathically share with you what I know or feel about horses. Some women are gifted writers who happen to be horse women. I'm a horse woman who writes. For me, working with horses is like breathing; natural, reflexive, and usually effortless until something interrupts the normal rhythm. All champion horse women still have to work at it and so do best-selling authors. Technically, I'm both, but the word thing is far more of a challenge than the horse thing.

Horses captured my heart and imagination before I had conscious memory. If scientists ever map the human genome more precisely, I suspect the horse-crazy gene is attached in close proximately to the one that also makes me a dachshund-girl. I love all dogs and animals, but once you've lived with a dachshund, there's no substitute.

My horses and I are getting on in years. The highlights in my red hair aren't really blonde, but silver. Most of my equine career revolved around young horses, newborn foals too wobbly to stand, too frustratingly uncoordinated to nurse once all four legs pointed mostly north and south, needing one of a hundred kinds of support until nature took over. I witnessed the pratfalls and beauty of live-cover breeding, guided hormone laden young stallions through the finer and more productive points of meeting mares, acting quickly when the unexpected happened, and stifling disrespectful laughter when Mr. Stud Muffin lacked focus or coordination.

Clients allowed me to train and show their babies, youngsters, two-year-olds, young adults, and some horses with a little more experience. For years I balanced the dueling challenges of training, breeding, and showing stallions. The horses and I learned together. I'm still learning. Today, I'm a mature woman working with mature horses. You could say I run an elder-stable, with all but my youngest roughly the same age in horse years as I am in human years.

Older horses have their own challenges and opportunities. They're not as hormonal, reactive, or quick as youngsters, and keeping them healthy, sound, productive, and entertained requires a different set of tools. There's a lot about teaching, rehabbing, and developing my older herd that's similar to the youngsters of my past because I'm still human and they're still horses. After thirty years I still love touching velvet noses, seeing my reflection in luminous brown eyes, and watching the dance of equine ears. I'm excited, blessed, and aware that there's still far more I don't know than I do.

Senior Women and Senior Horses

If you, your horse, or both of you are of a certain age, I have good news for you. One of the most valuable gaits is the walk, which is why I've devoted two chapters to it. Even if you have perfect health, endless confidence, and your horse is spook-free, developing a great walk is important.

Even with restrictions, concerns, or history, you can still live your horse dream. No matter how talented you are, you'll never master all that's possible with a horse. No one will, and even if you don't ride, nothing else offers the thrill, challenge, frustration, soul-crushing and spirit-soaring possibilities of life shared with these mystical beings.

Why horses? What fuels your passion? Why are you reading this book?

If you're searching for the explanation, you'll discover how other women express their own fascination with horses.

Why horses?

What a question, almost as if there were another option.

"A man, I'm told, often retreats to a silent place to deal with his issues alone. But a woman often needs to talk things over with a willing partner to help her find her way. A woman needs a relationship with intimate sharing and loving acceptance...a place of safety and belonging for her true self to emerge."

Betsy Talcott Kelleher
Sometimes a Woman Needs a Horse

Why Horses?

"After the connection is made, words cease to exist."

Jennifer Sailaz

Brownie was gorgeous. Amazing. Huge. A brown horse with a brown mane and tail. What made him more special than any other horse is that little red-haired, freckle-faced, four-year-old me was going to ride him! Six decades later I still remember the barnyard and the country road it bordered. My first ride on a real horse was bareback, brief, and memorable.

I fell off.

Brownie stepped on me.

I was in love.

That wasn't the beginning of my love affair with horses. As far as I know, I was born with it. I rode ponies tethered to a type of merry-go-round at the Minnesota Freeborn County Fair later, but Brownie was my first non-imaginary horse experience. The grown-ups were horrified when I fell and got squashed.

Brownie did nothing wrong, and it never occurred to me to be scared. Or angry. Or cry. I'm a natural born horse-crazy girl and an evolved equine geek. Horses were my passion, my teachers, and still fill those roles today. They're no longer my livelihood, but horses still teach, inspire, challenge, and feed my spirit.

Horses make sense in a world that doesn't. I don't understand why people hate, argue, scheme, belittle, and harm one another. We humans can be quixotic, generous, hateful, loving, and nasty. Horses aren't that way. They're consistently *horse*. All of them. Delightful, comical, challenging, endearing, frustrating comedians and dramatists of the stable. Who wouldn't be captivated?

Horses have individual personalities, aptitudes, likes and dislikes, with endless ways of expressing them. A lifetime isn't long enough to experience all that horses have to offer. Women are particularly drawn to horses; a fact science can't explain. Just the thought of horses stirs the heart, imagination, and emotions.

> *"When asked to describe in three words what it means to win Badminton 2018, the world's most challenging and prestigious equestrian event, 38-year-old Jonelle Price - the first woman to take the title for a decade - knocked back a glass of champagne and answered, 'Dreams. Come. True'"*

For Jonelle, horses make dreams live. She sat on her first horse when she was eight. Years of babysitting, waitressing, and mowing lawns funded her horse passion. After twenty years of hard work, others began noticing the shape her dreams were taking. I imagine Jonelle lived her dream daily—throughout all the years of being an equestrian nobody because she shared her life with horses, and isn't that the essence of the dream?

Jane Smiley, author and horsewoman, offers her answer to "Why horses?"

> *"I learned why 'out riding' alone is an oxymoron. An equestrian is never alone, is always sensing the other being, the mysterious but also understandable living being that is the horse. All equestrians, if they last long*

enough, learn that riding in whatever form is a lifelong sport and art, an endeavor that is both familiar and new every time you take the horse out of his stall or pasture."

Elyssa Doner, founder and instructor at Idyle Wild Farm, says of horses, "women watch with a sense of wonder... knowing that there was simply something more —something mysterious and mystical, that lived in the Realm of Horse."

More than anything else, horses make us *feel* by offering a primal connection unchanged since the Garden of Eden. God made man to be stewards and caretakers of the animals in the Garden. Relationship with horses isn't only possible, but amazing and purely natural.

———————

I live in a barn with horses. Our kitchen coffee pot is roughly nine feet from the horse stalls. The horses always know when I'm coming through the door. Ears come to attention as eyes focus on the door. It opens, and there I am! The moment I enter the horse side of our home every equine eye locks onto my face. I had to earn that focus and make sure I continue to deserve it. That irreplaceable gift is always satisfying, often spiritual, and occasionally magical.

Horses learn the cadence of your footfall. They recognize your energy and spirit. My delight is knowing that in all the world, my horses know when it's me, a knowing that makes them secure and happy.

Sadly, it isn't that way in every barn. Some horses hear the footfall of their master with trepidation or fear. Others with complete indifference because the human in their life is disconnected, disinterested, and unimportant.

17

Tragically, some horses hear their master's approach and prepare for the fight they know is coming. Survival is tough, especially when you have no freedom to leave. Horses seldom have a choice in where they live and with whom.

Why horses? Because I've worked with bored, fearful, or retaliatory horses who still chose to respond. Establishing a connection may take hours, days, or years - but eventually the horse commits. Trust has a new beginning and together we are transformed. Nothing is better than knowing that your dedication, love, and passion changes lives; the horse's and your own.

Earning a horse's devotion is the culmination of endless commitment. If you're a horse girl like me, once you've tasted it you can't give it up. The love of horses motivated me to get involved with horses, but it's their response that keeps me here doing what I do even when it's 112 degrees and humid and my sweat is sweating. Or below zero and blowing, fingers without feeling, bracing in a ridiculous number of layers to stay warm, making sure all is well in the herd. Horse women do what they do when they feel fabulous and even when they don't. What matters is the relationship, the bottomless well of life with horses, producing sips of sweet water non-horse folks can't imagine.

What matters most to horses isn't so much what you do as why you do it.

Age affects everyone. I'm officially *elderly*, but I mess with horses because there's still so much I don't know and I haven't even scratched the surface of what's possible. The challenge horses offer is as real to me today as it was decades ago. The details are different, but my desire to learn is as strong as ever. Horses teach me and through them I teach others. Besides, horses don't believe in silly labels like youthful, elderly, or geriatric.

Critter-crazy from birth, my childhood recurring dreams featured colored ponies frolicking in our suburban back yard. Not colored like Appaloosas, Paints, or Palominos, but like blue, red, green, purple, and yellow. I never thought about that until now, but maybe that was the beginning of my love for horses of different colors.

Why horses? For me it's relationship. Security and love were scarce during my childhood. I never worried about hunger or being homeless, but few people really knew me or seemed to care. At four I thought I was adopted. People weren't trustworthy and I sure didn't understand them. Animals made sense. They treated the odd little girl I was with kindness, welcoming me with open hearts and warm paws or hooves of acceptance. Which, I suspect, is why my tumble off Brownie as a four-year-old brought delight, not tears.

The true measure of success is found in time spent together with those you love; treasuring the moments when communication happens without conscious effort. There is a special bond of connection between women and horses. There is delight even in the mundane, doing chores that done well today must be done again tomorrow and the day after. Drudgery isn't what you do, but your perspective of what you do. Caring for horses and family can be a job or a joy, depending on why you do it.

The best motivation for life with horses is love; my love for them and theirs for me. It's worth everything.

There's no way to explain it to someone who isn't in love with horses. But for those who are, no words are necessary. Eyes meet, a small knowing smile curls the lips, and with a slight nod of recognition and understanding; you know that you are sisters in the Realm of Horses.

———————

"I was drawn to horses as if they were magnets. It was in my blood. I must have inherited from my grandfather a genetic proclivity toward the equine species. Perhaps there's a quirk in the DNA that makes horse people different from everyone else, that instantly divides humanity into those who love horses and the others, who simply don't know."

A.J. Hamilton

Free

"The shy creature who claimed painting and reading were her favorite pastimes had just bolted across the yard like a seasoned jockey atop a Thoroughbred. She might have inherited her mother's grace and manners, but the woman rode like her outlaw father.

Maybe better."

Karen Witemeyer, *Stealing the Preacher*

Lynn Baber

Will They Come Back

The first time I turned our horses out into the grass pastures at our Texas ranch I wondered, *"Will they come back?"*

Most of the relationship (training) work I do with horses is at liberty, meaning they don't have to participate if they don't want to. I want to earn a horse's attention and deserve his willingness. Liberty work sometimes means taking risks.

Nestled in the High Sonoran Desert, my Arizona training facility was fifteen miles north of Phoenix, with mountains visible on every side, and no grass. The largest paddock was just over a third of an acre, every square foot of dirt visible, with the horses never far from the gate.

The new paddocks in Texas were pastures, each one ranging from eight to fifteen acres. None of the horses we moved from Arizona ever experienced such open space, much less the freedom it offers. Every horse was born and raised in show barns. Precisely arranged on ten acres, my Arizona facility sported two arenas, one open, one covered; three round pens, two hot walkers, three show barns plus additional covered pens, a trail course, sliding track, quarter-mile jogging track, two homes, and miscellaneous buildings.

Not only were the Texas pastures huge by comparison, but there was a significant temptation factor. There were no grass pastures large or small in our part of Arizona; every paddock is a dry lot. The Texas paddocks were huge, adorned with oak trees, and carpeted with grass. Our horses never experienced fence-to-fence grass before but I couldn't let them stay out on it forever. Except for the breeding stock, the horses had to go back to the barn. When I went to the gate the first day to call them in, I admit feeling an unexpected sense of insecurity. This was an unknown.

"Would they hear my voice? Will they come when I call?"

It's easy to be present and focused in familiar confined spaces, but when you give horses or people expanded freedoms, the odds often change. Freedom adds options.

Maybe the horses came to me in Arizona because the only food was in the barn. In Texas pastures, food was everywhere. The horses didn't have to come.

But they did. They know my voice and trust me. Isn't that love?

———

"My sheep hear My voice, and I know them, and they follow Me."

John 10:27

I Know Why the Old Horsewoman Sings

Andie Andrews

I know why the old horsewoman sings.

She sings in a voice gone raspy and low, worn by time and inhaled sawdust and by calling for her horses far afield where the grass holds sway. They lift their heads, waiting for the familiar trill of their own names, each one a melody she has composed in her heart that floats into their tilted ears and moves their feet toward home.

She sings to calm the spooky one, whose wide eyes and rigid body soften at the vibrato that massages his skin and encourages him to blink at the sound of love.

She sings to lift the sagging back of the elderly one, whose top line bore the weight of careless riders with countless things to prove, whose eyes meet hers in understanding that she has carried her share of burdens too.

She sings to reach the aloof one, whose head shies at the lift of a hand but who yawns and leans into the soothing tones drifting through the iron bars of her equine mind and heart.

She sings to pass a rainy day, her feet shod in purple muck boots and propped on a bale of hay outside the stalls, delighting in the accompaniment of snorted breath and rhythmic munching that turns her song into a symphony.

She sings to rejoice in her glory days on horseback, in memories of soft greenswards and daunting, hardscrabble ridges that even still transport her to hallowed places of freedom, partnership, and peace.

She sings to dissipate the deep ache in her knees and the grief in her heart of knowing her physical strength dwindles like twilight, yet she raises her song all the more to welcome the timeless stars of beauty, joy, and wisdom a relationship with horses brings.

She sings because it forces her to breathe deeply, to become harmonious and fully alive with the horses in her midst, in the incredible, mystical, power of now.

She sings for horses everywhere, for the lame ones, for the abused and abandoned ones, for the young ones and the old ones, for the wild ones and for the wild at heart, her wobbly notes rising like incense, her songs a hymnal of prayer and praise.

She sings to offer thanks for a warm barn and cool water, for farmers and spring rain, for a loft filled with fragrant, green hay...and for her hard-won voice, gone raspy and low.

Yes, I know why the old horsewoman sings.

Andie is a sensitive and expressive poet and author. I don't remember how we met, but she has enriched my life and soul with her gift of words and the way she gives expression to the innermost truths of my love for horses.

Life with Horses

Jennifer was accomplished, motivated, and successful. We met because she wanted to buy a horse. At fifty-three, she was ready to live her childhood fantasy, sharing morning breaths with her equine partner, answering a nicker intended only for her ears, galloping with her hair swept out behind, feeling the tickle of the mane brushing her hands. She wanted to share life with a horse. It was time for her dream to grow wings and live.

Like me, a younger Jennifer watched *Fury*, *My Friend Flicka*, *Roy Rogers*, and even *Mr. Ed*. She read every horse book and dreamed of combing tails and kissing soft noses. Her dreamscapes included bareback rides through meadows and streams, glimpsing a bit of what centaurs must feel; human upper and equine lower. This was her time; time to get a horse of her own.

Usually there's a very practical side to dreams that you don't expect. When it comes to horses that's true in spades. Before introducing Jennifer to any horses I needed to know a little more about her. My goal was placing each horse in the right home, even when it meant not making a sale.

"Do you work, Jennifer? What do you do for fun?"

"When the kids left for college I got involved in real estate. Now I'm a broker and can finally afford to have a horse. Other than that, my husband and I play Bridge with friends and I go to Bible Study Wednesday evenings."

"Wow, it sounds like you're already busy! Do you

have grandchildren?"

"Oh, yes! Three so far and another on the way."

"Congratulations! Do they live close to you?"

"All three kids live less than an hour away, so we see them often."

"Where will you keep your horse? Do you have a place at home or are you going to board?"

"I'd love to get a little horse property. There are some good buys right now, so I could have my horse at home and make a good investment."

"You're in the right business for that. What's your horse experience so far?"

"I took lessons when I was fifteen and rode in a few schooling shows. Since then I haven't had the time or money for horses."

"What do you want to do with your horse?"

"I'd love to compete at little shows and maybe use my horse to help others. I know there's lots of equine therapy and ministry programs. Nothing fancy. Mostly I want to have my very own horse. "

"Jennifer, I'm going to tell you something I've told many people. You can have a horse or you can have a life, but you can't have both. It sounds like you're already pretty committed. Have you thought about what you're willing to give up so you can add a horse to your life?"

Jennifer didn't answer because she wasn't prepared for the question.

Girls and horses go together like moss on a north-facing rock. Some of us come late to the party but have just as much fun. I didn't own my own horse until I was in my early 30s, yet still managed a lengthy horse career, becoming a World and National Champion breeder and trainer, show judge in the USA and Europe, and expert witness in court.

But I had to give up a few things, like my career as a business consultant and motivational speaker. I naively thought I could still accept bookings and learn to train horses and manage a barn. I thought wrong. Nothing of value comes without a cost.

My husband and I also gave up the freedom to travel, even to visit the kids and grandchildren. Livestock can't be locked up until you get back in town like cars or motorcycles. During the years when I had employees I could leave without concern, but our years in Texas have been self-serve; no staff. Horses and cattle need to be fed, watered, inspected, and protected every day. We missed out on a lot of family time.

Life with horses comes with loads of baggage and vacuums up scads of resources like time, energy, and cash. Jennifer had the energy and cash but was short on time and lacked the knowledge I learned from trial and error. The biggest lessons usually come from screw-ups. Part of what clients pay for is experience, taking advantage of my costly mistakes so they don't have to repeat them. That saves time, blood, even more money, and maybe the health or relationship with the horse of their dreams.

When it comes to horses, not having enough knowledge is seldom a deal-breaker. If you have enough time, energy, and cash, instruction is widely available for those who are motivated enough to find it. No one knows what they don't know. Wisdom includes the awareness that you lack knowledge.[2] Jennifer came to my barn because a friend recommended me. She knew I wouldn't sell her a horse just to cash her check. My goal is happy clients. Happy owners usually have happy horses, which, I admit, is my greatest concern. Trust is earned, not only with horses, but with clients.

For most women, the biggest barrier to life with horses is time or other restrictions. Unlike cars or cats, horses require a healthy and balanced relationship. Horses need you to show up, sometimes more than once a day depending on where you stable your horse and with whom. Who will meet every equine need God built in when you're not there? Horses are born looking for a herd.

Health or advancing age isn't always the barrier you might expect. Horses don't care if you ride them. I've never seen a horse pull his owner to the tack room and beg for a saddle and bridle. Blind women ride. Wheelchair-bound women ride and enjoy ground work. Possibilities of relationship are endless, as long as they make sense to the horse.

Few things are as sad as a lonely horse. My heart breaks when I drive by a pasture with one horse. No herd means no security and no one who cares. Given the choice, most horses would choose companionship over regular meals. The lack of food and water kills the body, but solitary confinement kills the equine soul and spirit.

Without lots of time you can free up, you may not be able to own a horse unless your plan is to leave it with a trainer. If not, don't give up easily, because there are options like lessons or shared leases. Equine therapy barns

---

[2] Proverbs 1:1-4

offer amazing experience for everyone, especially volunteers. Maybe you could exercise other busy women's horses.

Do you have energy to spare? I've reached the age where I don't have as much energy this year as I did last year, a trend that will doubtlessly continue. Training and caring for dozens of horses used to be my norm. Now it's a chore to ride three and mess a little with another two. If you don't have energy reserves, what will you stop doing to free up what a horse requires? Don't take this lightly. Your horse still needs to be fed and watered even when you have the flu or a sprained ankle. Can you tough it out or is there back up at home? What's Plan B?

Horses aren't cheap. Even if you have a hundred acres of lush grazing grass behind the house to provide a yummy 24/7 salad bar for a horse, there are more major expenses to consider. If you're adding one horse, maybe you need two? Horses need herdship. That means you're responsible to provide it. It's either you or another horse, a goat, or maybe rent-a-kid. Two horses are better than one but twice as expensive.

Do you have cash to spare? If not, what are you willing to give up to fund your new horse habit? The cheapest part of life with horses is the purchase price. Serious cash expenditures kick in once the bill of sale is filed.

One of the biggest circuits I judged in Phoenix was open; meaning that no particular breeding or registration papers were required. Other than that, the rules were the same as breed shows. Some of the largest classes I judged were in this circuit because the awards for each show and at year end were spectacular. Competition was fierce. I remember one Western Pleasure class with three cuts! That meant I had to judge three separate classes as eliminators to make the size of the final class manageable.

At the end of each class the announcer reads off the names of the horse and rider teams who placed for ribbons or awards. One horse had the perfect name, *Adios Dinero*, which means Goodbye Money. For the economically minded that sums up life with horses quite well. You can spend your money on diamonds, exotic vacations, designer duds or hay burners. They're all expensive, but only one loves you for no other reason than because you're you.[3] You can forget all the rest because horses aren't impressed. So maybe horses are a good investment after all.

Jennifer didn't buy a horse that day. Like many women, she had more than one dream and sometimes you must choose. Jennifer had a wonderful marriage, grandchildren, and a rewarding career. Thankfully, she wasn't willing to put her husband, employees, family, or walk with Christ on hold to get a horse of her own.

Maybe this day wasn't her day, but that doesn't mean the right day won't come later. One of Jennifer's granddaughters might be as horse-crazy as she is. One day she may sell her business or do real estate part time. I expect Jennifer will still enjoy a season with horses because her dream lives on.

---

[3] Ecclesiastes 2:10-11, 4:9

Relationship

"The cover photo of "The Breath of Horse Crazy" makes me think of one starlit summer night when I perched on the water tank, just resting, and our herd of four horses gathered around me in a circle. Their breath mingled with mine and they quietly dozed together. I remember feeling suspended in Peace. It was one of the best, most healing prayer moments I've ever experienced."

Stephanie Bianchi

Everything of value links to a relationship. The difference between an acquaintance and a BFF is the nature and quality of relationship. Horses are all about relationship, born understanding life in a herd, knowing that the extended family will meet every important need.

Some folks are satisfied with rent-a-horses, paying for an hour of saddle time, neither making nor expecting promises. There's nothing wrong with that, it fills a need and employs horses trained to work without personal attachment. Women seek a deeper, more satisfying connection. There's a special wonder and joy when a horse offers you his personality, heart, power, and trust. There's no comparison between waltzing with a paid professional and slow-dancing to the single beat of two hearts with the man of your dreams.

Horses live, move, and think at the speed of trust, and unlike some people, horses can't be bought. They give honestly or not at all. You can't rent or borrow a horse's commitment. Horses understand focus. Desire. Trust. The end of the rainbow for horse-crazy ladies is transformation —becoming more than you were alone.

Horses tell you things about yourself you don't already know. Horses are as true to their nature as you are, never believing things about themselves that aren't real. Few of us can say the same thing without crossing two fingers behind our backs.

Elyssa Donner observes that, "Horses have an inherently unique ability to show us who and how we are being in the world. Just by being in their presence, horses can open our eyes to what I like to call "blind spots" — behaviors that we display without even realizing it — and consequently help us to see ourselves in ways we may not have been able to see otherwise."

Horses are experts at reading body language. We aren't as fluent and often make mistakes. Horses interpret body language the way horses always interpret body language unless they learn new definitions. For instance, walking toward a horse's head with your arm outstretched is a classically aggressive move. My horses interpret it differently. I teach them that this aggressive move from me is the International Symbol for Pet. At least that's what I call it. My horses see me approach; confidently cadenced, arm outstretched, looking them square in the eyes—and they settle. Eyes soften, lips relax, and heads lower to meet my fingers. They know they're about to get loved on. Affirmed. Rewarded.

Horses respond to physical nuances most humans miss. They live in the moment, process everything around them, and offer to teach us to do likewise. If your horse isn't giving you the response you expect, you didn't ask correctly.4 It's that simple.

Dealing with people and horses is either relational or some kind of twisted contest, every meeting designed to get the win, to further one's personal goal or serve some psychological need. Control is all about who has it and who wants it. Relationship seeks to maximize the other, to leave a win in both columns, and results in a net positive for everyone. Interaction based on control results in a winner and a loser. It's adversarial, mean, and something no horse-crazy woman dreams of.

In life with horses, there is no yesterday or tomorrow, but always and only today. Always leave the barn stronger, more peaceful, richer, and more in love.

Every journey is personal. My methods focus on each individual horse and human, not any particular discipline, philosophy, or doctrine of horsemanship. Horses who bless us with relationship don't read books on Natural Horsemanship, Classical Dressage, or clicker training. Horses haven't even read the Bible, yet they aren't conflicted about the nature of their Creator, the spirit He gave them, or the plan by which they live.

At its best, every training method that emphasizes relationship and horse sense over dominance establishes communication with a horse that earns its trust, obedience, and willing participation in a hybrid of leader-follower and partnership relationship. The words *must, should, always,* and *never* have little use when speaking about relationship. Horses read your body language and your energy and spirit. Come to a horse relationship with an agenda of "My way or the highway" and you'll have a fight

---

⁴ James 4:3

on your hands. Approach a horse with simple love, offer worthy leadership or partnership, and the horse will respond in spades.

Horses can smell fake at a hundred paces. They know the difference between someone playing a role, trying out a line, and authentic character. It's better to be real and make a mistake with your horse than appear smoother than silk with a cold heart. None of us is who we aspire to be, but most of us are willing to put in the effort because we care. The cobblestones, bricks, blocks, and footings of relationship with a horse add up over days, weeks, and years to form what is amazing, inspirational, and in some ways even supernatural.

Relationship is fluid, never static, moving from progress to regress and back to progress again. Trouble brews when forward movement slows or stops. The currency of leadership is trust—faith in the other's constancy and commitment. The power of habits, common sense, and fear disappear in a soft voice that says, "Follow me."[5] The root of transformative relationship is faith.

The ultimate test of a horse's faith in its master is reflexive, spontaneous obedience in the face of obvious danger. Horsemanship isn't about tradition, discipline, maneuvers, or philosophy. It is about vivid, personal, all-encompassing relationship to you. How much time do you spend thinking about how to *do* horses instead of observing or simply keeping company with them? *Being* is the path to wisdom, insight, and understanding that feeds the spirit of women who love horses. The best way to learn *horse* is from one.

---

[5] Matthew 9:9, John 8:12 and 10:4

Commitment

"No reserve. No retreat. No regret."

William Borden

When people ask me what I do to transform a horse I answer, "Whatever it takes."

"How long does it take?"

"As long as it takes."

I withhold nothing. My definition of commitment is "no matter what." There are no deal breakers or excuses. What's promised must be delivered. One of the greatest skills I've learned over the past thirty years is knowing what and how much to promise. If you can't deliver, don't say you can. It's that simple—which isn't at all the same thing as easy. Do you know your limitations? Can you foresee the snags that may crop up tomorrow or next week?

Horses have one big question, "Can I trust you?"

———

"You're not getting by me, buddy."

The steel-shod hoof was on a collision path with my face. It belonged to a rearing three-year-old stallion. I saw the hoof as if in slow-motion, framed by a clear deep-water blue Arizona sky, above my head but sinking fast. I don't remember what caused the saddled stud to rear, but I do remember standing my ground. Waiting for impact, knowing it might hurt, but positive I wasn't going to move.

I owned the ground. I fully occupied my space and prepared to defend it. Offering leadership to a stallion is seldom a physical contest, proving who's bigger, stronger, or faster. It's a mental game. If I tell a stallion that I own the universe, including the little spot of sand I stand on, I'd learned that I better own it no matter what.

Slow motion allows you to register and consider every detail. You know what's happening and what's coming, totally present in the moment with time to react. Before you think I'm a total idiot, I assure you I can duck, evade, or regroup in a split-second. That being said, there are moments in my career I'll never forget because of the magnitude of the lesson I learned. This was one of those moments. I also believe there was an angel on duty.

The stallion's front left hoof somehow connected to the inside of my right upper lip but never touched the outside of my mouth, just the inside. I don't know how that's possible and I never felt the impact. My mouth isn't as symmetrical as it used to be, the scar hidden unless I turn my lip inside out, which I've never had reason to do. Who walks around with their lip turned inside out anyway?

I could have moved but was determined to hold the ground I'd worked so hard to gain. When horses misbehave you must weigh your options and the relative benefit or cost of each one. Life with stallions, more than mares or gelding, frequently requires you to take a stand. I did. It worked out.

Not long afterward, after being saddled by my assistant trainer, that same stallion got away. He'd skedaddled and went for a little run around the place.

When I saw him running loose, I followed him, finding him at the end of the back driveway. We always locked the gate to the road unless we expected a semi delivery of hay, so his only option was to come out the same way he went in.

I stood in his way.

Hindquarters to the road, he looked at me. I looked at him. The driveway created a kind of alley, fenced on one side by the perimeter of the property and the other by my big outdoor arena. He stood about sixty feet away from me at the end of a twenty-foot-wide lane. Watching me.

I knew he was thinking, "Can I get by her?"

Then it got interesting. I didn't have as much as a lead rope with me. The stud outweighed me by a thousand pounds, but we knew each other, with relationship history to draw from as we considered our options. He knew I never break promises and what I say will happen always happens.

I stood my ground when he reared; he remembered. So, did I.

Horses know what you think and feel. I didn't know how I'd stop him if he charged but I knew there was no other option. He didn't. Don't try this at home! It was a calculation I made based on experience with this and many other horses. Thankfully, I calculated the odds correctly.

Commitment means "no matter what."[6] Faith grows

---

when commitment is challenged and refuses to yield. Stallions test humans the same way they challenge other stallions in the wild. They need to know what's what, who's in charge, and whether they're the leader or a follower. When you set reasonable boundaries in stone, most stallions willingly get along as part of their innate instinct for survival and herd relationship.

Wishy-washy doesn't work and indecision can get you killed. Use ultimatums sparingly because you must defend every line in the sand *no matter what*. Stallions differ from mares and geldings and are not suitable for everyone. They can be gentle as bunnies or as dangerous as a Tyrannosaurus Rex. Even the sweetest bunny can be obnoxious or dangerous in the wrong circumstances. I know, because I brought home a young rabbit in 1978 on his way to someone's dinner table and gave him to my dachshund for a pet. The pooch and rabbit were best friends, except on days when the bunny beat up his bigger buddy. Go figure.

Putting your swollen ego into a corral with a stallion is a recipe for disaster. No matter what happens to you, the horse will probably get the worst end of the experience. The downside for everyone involved is too great to take unnecessary chances. Unless you *need* a stallion, please don't get one.

I don't say that because I think stallions are bad, but because I love them. They're more vulnerable to abuse than other horses because people don't know how to relate to them in positive ways. When things go south, horses almost always pay the price.

Endless Commitment—Delayed Result

If I ever thought that well-planned progressive training sessions work with every horse, Ace is the exception.

During my career I was blessed with the luxury of training each horse as an individual, allowing me to learn or invent ways to work with difficult or special needs horses. Ace inspired me to figure out more ways to relate to him than any previous horse because none of the ones I already knew brought success.

Ace didn't respond to anything the way I expected. He was unpredictable, suffering from dissociative disorder, mentally leaving the planet when stressed, a disturbing complication when I was on his back. Earth and Ace didn't connect, let alone Ace and me. He was emotional, reactive, inconsistent, and volatile. He was also sweet, funny, interested, and asked for attention. Nothing about Ace proceeded in an orderly fashion from A to Z. He hopped from H to Z, reversed from E to A, and mixed letters together in ways that stymied me.

No normal training program worked with Ace. It would be relationship or nothing. I had to invent new ways to communicate with Ace and motivators that meant something to him. More than anything else, I had to commit. For the long term. Forever if that's what it took, and I feared it might.

Since forever comes anyway, why not spend part of my journey with Ace? So, I committed to the relationship.

Horse training is boring, with countless hours of nothing much except fellowship and the pursuit of better communication. Showing affection and commitment until your horse believes in you.

Every horse relationship isn't till death us do part. All relationships aren't precious or magical. If, after I've done all I can do and the horse chooses not to willingly engage, I remain a good steward but shake off the dust[7] and move on. Not every horse is a fit for you and you aren't the right partner for every horse. It's not personal, it just is.

The difference between transformative relationship and those that fall short is the level of focus and commitment each brings to the party. Relationship always suffers when one party fixates on "I, me, mine", whether it's with God, horses, or one another.

What commitment are you willing to make to your horse? Will you give your life? Maybe literally? If not, figure out where your commitment ends, because it matters. You can't expect your horse to offer greater devotion, commitment, precision, or concentration than you do. Horses read your spirit and intention. Never lie or make a promise you can't or won't keep. An honest seventy percent commitment is far better than a counterfeit one hundred percent.

If your goal is amazing relationship with a horse, what assets *can* you commit? What assets *will* you commit? What's your limit?[8]

Journey

We rescued Journey from a kill pen. All I knew about him when I bought him was what his right profile looked like above his legs. What I got was a problem. Some horses end up in the kill pen by pure circumstance. Others are sent there purposefully. That was Journey. Once home we began working; slowly, methodically, consistently.

---

[7] Matthew 10:14

[8] John 10:11

One day, after four months of working five and six days per week, Journey stood saddled and tied in his stall patiently waiting his turn, the same as he did without incident every day. We were still doing ground work because the full extent of Journey's demons had already revealed themselves. At least I thought they had.

Journey was quiet. Calm. I walked in, spoke to him, and reached for the lead rope. He exploded, bucking as he bolted from his stall, knocking me flat on the stall floor, charging over my head as he escaped to the covered pen. My husband yelled, "Lynn! Are you okay?"

"Yes."

"Do you know how close his feet came to your head?!?!"

It wasn't really a question, he was reacting to what he witnessed and what might have happened. My husband went into rescue mode. Journey was still bucking. My barely there knee and my replaced knee took the brunt of the slam but taking care of Journey came first. I couldn't leave him in fear. I promised him I'd never do that. If I broke a promise now, the road ahead would be longer than ever.

"Would you throw me my knees?" My *knees* are black Professional Choice knee braces for riders. I didn't think I'd be able to do what I needed to without them. I still wasn't sure, but I had to try. Twenty minutes later Journey was calm, working happily at all three gaits, and loved the hugs he got when I untacked him. No drama as far as he was concerned, which was precisely my goal. It was just another lesson that ended on a high note.

I hit the shower. After inspecting the damage, I pulled out the beautiful thigh-high compression stockings I got when my right knee was replaced and went on a week of rehab. My knees needed time to recover. So did my emotions.

The next day I had a talk with God I never expected to have. I wanted permission to quit because I was afraid, something I didn't really think was possible. I was obviously wrong about that, and permission to jump ship didn't come. I've discovered that the lessons I teach horses are also lessons intended for me. This one was a doozie. Commitment means keeping your promises, even when it's hard, even if you're afraid. Because breaking a promise is not an option.

Relationship isn't always easy, but without the surges of emotion and heart-lessons they bring, life would be too sterile to endure.

Credibility Score

Buying, saving, and even breathing seems to mess with your credit score. Anything you do seems to raise or lower it. Every relationship has a credibility score. You have one with your horse, a snapshot of where you are today. It doesn't reflect where you were last year, nor does it predict where you might be in the future.

It communicates what's real today. If your score is hot, keep doing what you're doing. If it isn't, maybe you need to see what you can do to bump it up.

We waited for someone special to arrive the first week of December 2017. One of Sky's boys we last saw eighteen years ago was coming home. We broke our rule of "No More Horses" when we learned that his loving mom of all those years couldn't keep him.

I'd just hired folks to take down the rails between two stalls so Journey's would be larger, and we wouldn't have an empty one. Because you know what happens when you have an empty stall—someone moves in. Instead of taking down the rails we prepared a welcome home for *Sky to a Q*, aka Q. Two days before the transport was due to arrive his stall was spotless and fresh, his feeder removed from the wall for a full wash.

Who else waited for Q? His full brother, Ace. His half-brother, Shiner, and Journey and Bo.

And me.

I bred Q's mother to Sky, welcomed him into the world, and kept him company at weaning time. I taught Q his manners, how to walk on a treadmill, then prepped and showed him in his baby futurity. He's the only youngster I harnessed and let pull a training cart as a long yearling because he was smart, willing, and bored. He demanded something more to do, so I obliged. I drove him from the ground, but he pulled the cart like a pro.

As a two-year-old I started him under saddle and prepared him to be a show horse and member of someone's family. Susan bought him when we sold him at three. Her doctors told her she'd be in a wheelchair within a year, but she had a different plan. She added Q to her life and is still walking today. I doubt he showed much, but he carried his owner countless miles in arenas and on trails. Our reunion wouldn't be possible if Susan (an R.N.) hadn't nursed him back to health after a serious alligator attack. No one expected him to pull through. He did, but I hear he doesn't like water.

Horses are devoted and inspire the same in us. Susan loved Q and did what everyone said was impossible to save him. Q loved her right back. What's possible is often underestimated without figuring in the power of love.

Most of you know how hard it is to part with a beloved equine. Whether via the Rainbow Bridge or other circumstance, saying goodbye is hard. Really hard. I've prayed for Q's mom. They shared most of a lifetime together, but Susan let him come back to us because she loved him.

Meeting Q as an adult was exciting. I've never brought a smart, opinionated, spoiled geriatric gentleman back into work. The biggest question I had was, "Will he remember me?" Four months and lots of food and rehabilitation later, I realized that there are times in a relationship when you must step back and get hold of yourself. Return eyes of accusation from whoever is bugging you to the mirror, and settle your breath, spirit, and temper.

Horses push your buttons just like people. On rare occasions it's purposeful, but usually it's an emotional reaction to what's happening. I seldom exercise emotionalism, whether positive or negative, with horses or people. Frustration and anger are poor leadership characteristics.[9] Telling your horse, child, friend, or acquaintance to "Trust me" is never as meaningful as BEING trustworthy. Acting impulsively proves us liars.

But there are times.

A few months after Q came home, I dismounted before the lesson was over because he was a complete idiot. My feet hit the dirt and I tipped toward irritation.[10] I am shamefaced to report this, but I may even have said, "You have no idea who you're messing with, buddy."

While marching back to the barn for a longe line, I recognized my emotion. Stifled it. And figured out my next best action. Q expected me to get after him as punishment, but that's not my way. We walked back to the scene of his poor behavior and I asked him to—

"Please walk."

Quietly. Calmly. Free of emotion.

Except relief, that I'd caught myself before engaging in wrong behavior. That's the power of the Holy Spirit. Not

---

[9] Galatians 6:9

[10] Proverbs 14:29, Ecclesiastes 7:9, James 1:19-20

proving that I'm all that disciplined, but that God offers that much grace when you earnestly seek it.

The lesson went longer than planned but added strength to our foundation and saved what could have trashed my credibility score! It was good.

Oswald Chambers wrote, "Watch spiritual hardness, if ever you have the tiniest trace of it, haul up everything else till you get back your softness to the Spirit of God."

Since then, Mr. Q has come back to great weight, improved muscle tone and athletic ability, and learned to appreciate the rhythms of our barn. The vacuum I use to groom him is the same one I used when he was a baby, a yearling, a two- and three-year-old.

Q is back. I think he remembers. I know I do.

Titan

One of the last horses I took in training was a 16.2 hand massive paint gelding. He's one major reason I stopped accepting outside horses. Don't get me wrong, I loved my years training horses, coaxing boldness from anxiety, watching latent talent grow and produce championships, testing my skills with every new horse that came into my barn.

Titan was a gorgeous show horse turned out to pasture. He was successfully shown by a teen-age rider in conformation, Western, and English classes. Finding a horse equally gifted in all three areas is rare. Titan was, with the show record to prove it.

Teenagers grow up. Titan had too much time off and was offered for sale. After a season of convincing him that he had to return to work, he was sold to a younger rider who wasn't capable of managing his huge body or personality. Titan got away with all kinds of bad behavior before his owners pitched him out for a couple of years, then decided to sell him.

Titan went back to the same trainer for another tune up. This time he was completely convinced that he was retired. He resisted, argued, cheated, and bullied riders. Then one of my clients bought him.

When I met Titan, I thought I was there to check him out and give my opinion. The trainer representing the owners told me my clients already bought him and were only waiting on the pre-purchase. I wouldn't have selected him for the teen-ager who planned to ride him. He was a mess. Pretty. Impressive. And a pretty impressive jerk. An eight-hundred-pound jerk is annoying; a fifteen-hundred-pound jerk is hard work.

Titan moved into my barn for a tune-up, but it was more like an intervention. He didn't want to get along. He cheated. He objected. He acted out. I persisted.

Eventually Titan realized I meant what I said, didn't take no for an answer, and was always fair. One day he did a complete turnaround and gave me everything he had, which was considerable! He became a dream to ride and be around. I loved him. We'd worked it out together. He committed to relationship one more time.

His owner took a weekly lesson but was too timid and uncertain for this big horse with a bigger ego. Time passed and they started working together. It was time for Titan to go home.

I'd done my job. Titan did his.

Things don't always work out as we hope or plan. For

a while Titan and his owner came over for lessons. Until school and other interests took over. More than a year later Titan's owners called. They wanted to sell him. Could they bring him back for a tune-up?

"What's going on?"

"He hasn't been ridden in months because our daughter is afraid of him."

I asked all the appropriate questions and made a few suggestions. The folks weren't interested in investing anything else in Titan. He was right back where he was before I met him. Except he'd been through the wringer one more time. I felt horrible for him.

For the first time I felt horrible, period. I make a big deal about never lying to a horse.

"Trust me."

"I'll take care of you."

"Nothing will hurt you."

Titan gave me his trust. He committed. He believed me. I sent him home.

I lied.

I'd never thought about it that way before. The only way Titan would come back to me is if I could commit to keeping him. I'd have to buy him, but I didn't have the space or time. I don't know what happened to Titan and I probably don't want to. My time as a professional trainer was coming to an end. I didn't have the stomach to lie to another horse. Which meant I couldn't bring one more horse home I didn't intend to keep.

I couldn't face Titan. The credibility score I worked so hard to build was trashed. I made a promise and I broke it. As is usually the case, the horse pays the price.

Sometimes God changes our hearts in preparation for what comes next. I went from full-time equine professional to ministry and authorship within two years. There's absolutely nothing wrong with training client horses. I did it for years. I still work with outside horses, but I'm careful about how much I promise. They know that they are safe as long as I have the lead or the reins. Once I hand them back my promise ends. I don't know how they understand, but they do. Horses are amazing.

Credibility is too hard to come by. So is self-respect. I learned my lesson. Helping horse owners with their horses is my passion. You're welcome to come on over with yours —but I won't take another one in training.

Credible people are consistent and faithful. Your credit score reflects each late payment and every failure. Even things that aren't actually failures, like too many cards or too much debt. Your Credibility Score reflects every slip or failure to keep your promises perfectly. Every moment you spend with your horse either teaches something new or confirms lessons already learned.

Wrong is never right. Right is always right.

Let your "yes" be "yes" and mean it when you say "no."[11]

Nothing is a light matter to God. He says things for a reason. He means what He says. When He wants

---

[11] Matthew 5:37

something gone, we are to remove it even though no one walks that out perfectly. What keeps us on the narrow path is the knowledge that God means what He says. He won't wink and turn away. What He thinks is important is important to us.[12]

When you establish something as important to your horse—enforce it. Every time. Mean what you say. Don't wink and turn away because he's cute or you're not that bothered at the moment. Ignore it, and the horse learns you don't mean what you say. Respect generates respect. Your credibility is on the line every time you enter your horse's presence. Guard it as you would any precious jewel.

_____

[12] Psalm 105:8, 2 Chronicles 16:9,

My First Horse

My doctor said I was permanently partially disabled, a thirty-three-year-old ex-athlete finally sidelined by old knee injuries. Painful ones that never let me forget they were there and that they were ticked. My career was exploding, and I'd recently come off a long political campaign besides operating a new business. I was desperately in need of a no-impact outlet for my excess energy because even water exercises were ruled out. "Sit unless you have to stand," my doctor said.

My father was an airline pilot, so one Saturday morning I took a flying lesson. I suffered from Meniere's disease for years. If you're not familiar, that means an invisible force struck me to the ground, impaling my head with an imaginary spike until the attack passed. The world spun while my body lay motionless. I kept my eyes closed, not the slightest bit embarrassed when carried bodily out of some swanky joints. The small plane set my vertigo into overdrive. One lesson was plenty. Flying was off the table.

When I arrived home, I told my husband, "Well, I can't fly, so tomorrow I'm looking for a stable."

"Why are you looking for a stable?"

Which was a reasonable question. My husband and I were consultants. He had a busy actuarial practice and I was building my business and increasing bookings as a motivational speaker.

Why would I need a stable?

"For my horse."

"You don't have a horse."

"I will tomorrow."

By Sunday afternoon I'd found a stable, bought a horse, and had her trailered to the barn. My new horse was a three-year-old untrained solid-colored Appaloosa filly I named Arizona Sky. She was copper penny brilliant with a thick flaxen mane and tail. Too cute for words and she was mine.

My Uncle Art taught me to saddle, harness, ride, and drive horses before I was ten. My father promised me a horse the year I turned ten. Twenty-three years later I quit waiting for my dream to begin.

Sitting on horseback made sense. I rode with an older friend who had served in the U.S. Cavalry. Not the tank division, mind you, but the mounted-on-horses Cavalry. Batch was in his 80s, living in what I considered adult Disneyland with horses and a donkey. Resident deer, rabbits, and pets of every kind populated his acreage. Riding wasn't as problematic as getting off and walking.

After dismounting I hung onto the saddle horn, letting the horse support me until my legs decided to play again. There are times now when my horses have to support me. If I need to hang onto neck, wither, or back, they're happy to schlep me along until I can manage on my own.

Arizona Sky knew how to lead but was never ridden. If you know much about horses, you know that putting a green horse and inexperienced rider together is often a recipe for disaster. In my case, I had enough background to cover the basics and God had a plan.

Arizona Sky fascinated me.

Challenged me.

Humbled me.

Gave me courage.

Taught me humility.

Made me feel like Roy Rogers, and

Hugged like a champion!

I learned to be respectful and how to earn her respect. We learned from each other. She offered me a gift I'd given up on in this lifetime—a horse of my own.

Arizona Sky taught me the proper use of spurs. Bottom line, if your horse bucks, don't clamp your legs and feet on the horse if you're wearing spurs. She'll buck bigger and higher. Don't tell anyone, but it took two unplanned trips to the ground before I figured that out. Even the memories that came with bruises are delightful when the lesson learned is valuable and the relationship sweeter. I learned to respect Arizona Sky the same way she learned to respect me. I taught her tricks and she taught me things about horses I never imagined.

Winters in Nebraska get cold. When the ice on the walls was too thick Arizona Sky and I played in the indoor round pen. Some days we danced. Dancing is like heeling with a dog; no halter or lead rope. No matter what I did, how quickly I twirled or changed directions—right, left, forward, backward—Arizona Sky was supposed to remain at my right elbow. Our dance got increasingly fast and furious. I expected Arizona Sky to stop, back, roll right, swing left, faster and faster. She kept it up until she stopped and deliberately nipped my right elbow.

Then, looking directly into my eyes, with love, to make sure I got the message, she trotted to the perimeter of the round pen in self-correction. To be sure, there was a glint in her eye, a smirk on her lips, and a sassy flip to the end of her voluminous tail. She made her point. Arizona Sky wasn't mad or unhappy, but she clearly said, "I quit."

"Too much? Oops. My bad."

Another lesson learned.

It was hilarious, and I changed the lesson plan for the rest of the day. This remains one of the most memorable moments of my horse training career. Arizona Sky and I learned from each other. She offered me a gift I'd quit hoping for.

Rational people said I was too broken to train horses. Some thought I was too old to commit to a new lifestyle. I'm here to testify that rational people aren't always right.

If you're horse crazy like I am, the mere thought of *horse* is enough to send rushes of excited chemicals into your bloodstream and brain. As far back as I can remember, I wanted to learn about horses and had to touch each one I saw. I thought about horses. Dreamed about horses. Drew horses and played like a horse. My most prized possessions as a child were two Breyer models, one an Appaloosa and the other a Clydesdale.

We live in a barn, a big metal building with one end for our dwelling, the horse open pens/stalls and working rooms in the middle with a breezeway, and a small indoor working area on the far end. It's literally a fourteen-second walk from the chair at my desk to the stalls. It's also fourteen seconds from our bed to the stalls. Can you think of any sweeter set up?

Two sides of the residence part look out onto the pasture and arena. No matter where they are on the property, I can see my horses. They keep an eye out for us as well because we live together. I've always had a solid relationship with my horses. Our last barn was a hundred feet from the back porch. Sometimes I sat on the patio watching them nurdle in the pasture, marveling that they were mine and I was living my dream. I didn't expect much to change when we moved into the new barn with the horses except easier chores and less maintenance.

Saying I was wrong would be an understatement. Imagine the difference in the quality of relationship with a dog who comes in from his outdoor kennel in the morning and goes back at bedtime and the little scruffy one who demands your pillow every night in bed. You love them both, but one is a part-time love while the other affects every rhythm of your day.

The horses want to be where we are. They appear everywhere we do. If we're in the horse part of the barn and they're in the paddock, we end up with a volunteer committee.

"Whatcha doing? Can we help? Do you want to let us in? Where ya been?"

When we first moved in, I warned my husband that one day I would bring the horses inside the house. Why not? Our floor is the same as theirs except that our concrete is stained a deep chili color and roller stamped to be pretty. In the years since, I've changed my mind. They're as close to me as my husband is when we're in our respective offices; closer than it is from my office to our bedroom. They don't need to sneak into the house because they're already here.

Our barn sits well off the road, yet the label is easily visible to all driving north or south on a well-traveled road. Our building says H-O-R-S-E on the front in four-foot tall metal letters painted a deep teal color. Arizona Sky was the first to personify *horse* for me.

Do you remember your first love? Maybe you were a gawky tween, learning to navigate relationship with a member of the opposite sex. First impressions happen once, and your first love is unforgettable.

Arizona Sky was the first horse to join our family. The stable was twelve miles from our home. If I was in town, I was there. Every day. Riding horses isn't the same as owning one. Babysitting a child isn't the same as being a parent. You may employ someone to help care for your child, but you are in charge because you're the mom, making sure everything that needs to be done is done and done correctly.

A first baby is a totally new experience. You learn how to feed, clean, support, and recognize upset or potential illness. Becoming a mother for the first time explodes new emotions and concerns you'd never dreamed of. You obsess about dangerous corners, liquids, and potential hazards hiding in your home. Child-proofing becomes an art. You're the mom. I understand that second and subsequent children are far easier because you know the ropes. You know what's important and what isn't. What's fragile and what isn't. You guide bonding and relationship. Communication and socialization. Finally, teaching your child skills and utility.

Part of what I learned from Arizona Sky was how to care for the daily needs of a horse, to feel what she feels and recognize the signs when she's out of sorts. To understand what her expressive eyes communicated. To decipher what the tilt and twist of her ears meant.

How the hair of a horse's coat reverses direction in the most incredible way.

Where hazards and danger lurk.

What plants are good for horses and which ones can kill.

Judging moods without words.

The ins and outs of bonding and communication.

Setting boundaries and enforcing them.

To my surprise and joy, God had something in mind for me and horses. I spent most of the next three decades in the equine industry as a breeder, trainer, judge, and clinician.

It began with Arizona Sky. She was smart. Kind. Funny. And patient. She was my horse, my teacher, and my partner. I am better because of her. She not only provided answers but taught me how to figure out what questions to ask. God was training me with a shiny chestnut filly with a blonde mane and tail. My first horse.

Now the stage, the opportunity, and the responsibility are mine. Arizona Sky, my first equine love and special gift from a loving God.

Lynn Baber

The Upper Hoof

Who gets the upper hoof in your barn? Don't tell me you've never been totally irritated by a stinkin'-adorable equine bad actor.

Parents of children and horses understand dirt, sass, and being dumb on purpose. They've dried tears of both joy and frustration. It comes with the territory. Horses usually teach us how to behave more than we teach them.

Horses are simple, and often more effective getting what they want from us than we get from horses. Humans talk and pontificate, threaten and yell, while horses look at them with amusement or disdain. Horses lean on you. Ignore you. Step into your space—and your feet move. Not theirs. More horses step on people than people step on horses.

They win.

The more highly educated we are in the things of the world the less simple we get.[13] God may laugh at our delusions of grandeur unless His emotion is more one of disgust.

You can't fool a horse and you can't fool God.

---

[13] Psalm 19:7, 116:6, 1 Corinthians 1:27-29, Matthew 18:3, 19:14

First Impressions

Relationships always have a beginning and progress much like a dance, the continuing process of action and reaction. Entering the round pen with a new horse is like a chance meeting; once eyes meet something significant happens or an opportunity is lost.

How eyes meet sets the tone for the rest of the interaction. If someone held your head and forced you to look into someone else's eyes, what would you feel? Fear? Anger? Hostility? Resistance?

"You can trust me. It's okay."

"Then why is this goon holding my head hostage?"

Halters and ropes are restrictive. The horse has no freedom to respond, to choose, to think through the meeting. Why expect any response other than fear, anger, hostility, or resistance?

Round pens and liberty work are perfect partners.

Round pens offer two primary benefits; safety and freedom. The shape eliminates dangerous corners and lets you work at liberty. That means a round pen must be round and sturdy. Perhaps not perfectly round, but the closer it is to round the better it is for your horse's balance, development, and concentration.

Obedience at liberty is true obedience, like walking a tightrope without a safety net. Horses must have the freedom to choose to obey. Would Jesus have the same appeal if He roped and drug you into relationship? I chose Jesus the same way I want a horse to choose me. When He said, "Come," I came.[14] When He says "Follow," I followed. Not because I had no other choice, but because the invitation delighted me.

First impressions only happen once, but thankfully, horses have the most forgiving natures. They give you the opportunity for a do-over. More than once. We need second chances. Sometimes third and fourth ones as well. Offer your best whenever you're with your horse, but rest knowing that forgiveness is spelled, h-o-r-s-e.

Little girls don't dream about shotgun weddings, but about Prince Charming riding in on his majestic white horse to sweep her into happily ever after. Love is a choice. The only way to know if your horse will choose you is to give her the option to walk away.

Give her that. It's a beautiful beginning.

---

[14] Matthew 14:29, 19:14

Transformation

"For many young girls, having a horse of their own ranks high on the scale of importance, right up there with breathing."

Kim Meeder

Commitment establishes a beginning. Transformation is a process.

Doesn't every woman rescue a horse from a kill pen for her sixtieth birthday? An unseen horse at that, except for a small online photo of his left side that didn't even show his legs. We bought him without knowing a single fact about his history, experience, capability, or soundness.

The Appaloosa gelding, identified as Richard, was a looker the day he entered the kill pen and had his picture taken in the chute. That's the photo I saw. The before was much more impressive than the after.

We didn't need more mouths to feed or horses to care for. Days ticked off until I received notice that the Appaloosa gelding was out of time and shipping to Mexico. I asked my husband, "You know that Appy gelding we talked about two weeks ago? He's shipping this morning."

I expected my husband to say no, reminding me that we didn't need more animals, especially another horse. If he'd be the fall guy, making the tough choice, I could walk away guilt-free. He rolled his chair back from his desk, folded his arms on his chest, looked me square in the eye and said, "I think you'd better try to buy him."

Gulp.

I did not see that coming.

I bought him.

Now that Richard was mine, I wanted him out of that horrible place as soon as possible. After some frantic calls to people I'd never heard of before, I arranged to move and privately board him until I could get there. Apart from his color, the horse I picked up a few days later looked nothing like the horse in the photo. This one was thin, ribs easily numbered, hip bones sharp enough to hurt if you ran into them. His chest seemed alarmingly narrow and his unkempt front hooves almost touched. The only identification Richard came with were two auction stickers pasted to his skinny behind.

Instead of sending him to a friend for quarantine as planned, he went to the vet clinic. Ten days later he came home, softly yielding his head and neck to my fingers, finally tolerating being brushed by a stranger. Along the way I'd trimmed the worst from his overgrown hooves.

Our journey began and Richard got a new name, Journey.

For years I specialized in training and handling stallions. I trained, fixed, rehabilitated, and brought horses back into usefulness from bad behavior, bad experiences, and bad health. But I'd never run into a horse as damaged as Journey. It shouldn't have been a surprise. I knew the minute my husband said to buy him that something was up. This wasn't my first rodeo, or my first horse challenge orchestrated by Someone at the highest pay grade. I expected a lesson, but not a storm.

Journey was dangerous. His natural disposition was kind and reasonable, but whatever happened in the past broke his mind. What that means is he didn't react like a normal horse. He had triggers, that once pulled, resulted in explosions. Journey's natural sense of self-preservation blew up somewhere along the line. He was manageable—until triggered.

Remember, I was already sixty years old with a fake knee and a whole bunch of other questionable body parts. This didn't look promising. I'm good with rehabs and rogues, experienced with special needs horses and dogs, but Journey was something else altogether.

Several months into Journey's program I realized what I was up against and met with the Lord.

"I know how to do this. But I don't want to! I'm afraid."

I haven't been consciously afraid of anything since I don't know when. Yet here I was, owning that I was filled with fear. But the assignment wasn't pulled, and I wasn't excused. This journey was as much for me as for my troubled horse. Months after I started riding him, Journey backslid. I thought his trigger was buried deep enough to stay put if I did my job of maintaining balance, preparing for every ride, and staying the course. The trigger surfaced again.

I had to think about that for a while. What did it mean? Should it change the expectations? What was the message? Meeting the problem head on seemed the most reasonable option.

Part of Journey's gift is listening even when I'm not speaking aloud. I could think things when we worked at liberty and he'd do them. When I exhaled thirty feet from him, he'd softly drift from canter or rapid trot to a walk.

It was time to talk about commitment, so I called a meeting. I cradled Journey's head in my arms and said, "It's your choice. You can be Richard the rescue horse or you can be Journey, my partner, my friend, and my horse. But you can't be both. If you commit, so will I. If not, I'll find the best home for you I can."

Three years later, Journey is amazing. He does things for me no other horse ever offered to do. He's a good ride, fits me like a glove, and is reliable and confident.

I am no longer afraid. Neither is Journey.

We are transformed.

Transformation requires change. Nothing can become something other than what it is without change. Horse training is transformative, taking what exists and creating something new. The process can go either way, producing something better or something worse.

The nature of prayer isn't to get things or change our circumstances as much as it changes our attitude about the things we pray for. A wild horse may desire with its whole heart to return to wide open spaces. Right relationship won't put the horse back in the wild, but it may change the horse so he doesn't want to leave you. He's content, happy, satisfied, and confident, because he is home. He still has the nature of a horse, but no longer a wild horse. He is changed by relationship with you. Right relationship transforms wild horses into willing horses. From homeless to home free.

Education teaches skills but cannot change character when resistance to change is present. The requirements of transformation are *want to*, heart, commitment, and love.

A horse blessed by transformative relationship with a human may still live in the same stall as it did before, accepting the offer of worthy leadership, but its spirit, emotions, and future have dramatically shifted. Horses in right relationship with worthy leaders are not anxious, aggressive, or angry. They are content, bold, curious, and secure.

Among all the people on earth this horse knows its master.[15] What do I promise my horses? Joy, peace, provision, love, companionship, discernment, security, faith, fellowship, and blessing. Horses in a transformative relationship with a human may still perform the same basic maneuvers or routines they did before, but the how and why has shifted. Obedience is a gift given because refusal has become unthinkable.

Journey is obedient because he chooses me over everything else. Isn't that the sweetest part of the dream?

"Through the days of love and celebration and joy, and through the dark days of mourning – the faithful horse has been with us always."

Elizabeth Cotton

---

[15] John 10:2-5

Grace the Mustang

"Is my horse better off with someone else?"

Changes in income or health force women to consider the question. We're all getting older and horses are expensive. But what motivates this line of thought isn't concern for ourselves, but the love and concern for the welfare of the horse. Love always puts the needs of the beloved above our own.

Inability to care for a horse is one thing. Considering whether re-homing is a better option is quite another. Unable to find an answer to this specific question, Elizabeth sent me an email asking for guidance.

"Will you pray for me? Lynn, it seems that change is inevitable. A young trainer wants my mustang, Grace, to show at the Southwest Livestock Show. She wants to buy her, but Grace is my love. I'm in my early 70s but still blessed and able to care for and spend time with her. Grace is amazing, so I feel the trainer might do her more justice than I can. I don't want to think only of myself. Can you pray that I will understand God's will and His purpose in this situation?"

I replied to Elizabeth that change is inevitable but breaking up a relationship isn't. I continued:

Horses don't care what they do as long as they're with the person who loves and cares for them. Except for my rescue, every horse in our barn has champion breeding and is capable of performing at a higher level if they were with someone who still did that. Ask my boys if they would prefer standing in the spotlight or remaining unnoticed here, and they'd answer that this is home and we are their people. I have no idea what breeding Journey has, but he's got tons of ability. He'd give the same answer.

With all that being said, what are YOU feeling, Elizabeth? If you're concerned that Grace is too much for you, then consider it. If not, Grace loves the one who loves her. That's you. Potential isn't on a horse's radar, but love is. Grace isn't wasted with you. God's purpose is the same for all of us; that we focus on Him. Horses help keep us on track. Years ago, someone told me that Bo was wasted with me. He certainly is not! I learn from him daily and hear more from God because of him.

The world doesn't see through the same prism God does. Logic and love don't always walk hand in hand. God isn't impressed with training or competition not specifically related to His glory and our future with Him.[16] Horses aren't impressed with them either.

Trainers seldom stick with the same horse for long. What happens to Grace after the stock show? What about next year and the year after that? Mustangs usually change hands several times.

What's right for your family? For Grace? For you? That's all that matters.

If you wonder what happened to beloved Grace, she stayed home where she belongs.

---

[16] Acts 10:34

Balance

"Balance is the most fundamental factor affecting how well you ride. Balance is what determines your ability to teach the horse within his own ability. And balance, it seems, is what the horse searches for in a human companion. The horse is strong and sensitive, aggressive and affectionate, powerful and graceful. The horse searches for a companion who mirrors his or her own personality. So, to succeed with horses, and to be like horses, we must be balanced."

GaWaNi Pony Boy, *Of Women and Horses*

Asti could easily be a fantasy mare; tall, elegant, true black even in summer, with a fancy blaze, white stockings, and one beautiful cornflower blue eye in contrast to her deep brown one. Everything about her is gorgeous, her looks, conformation, gait quality, and her heart, which melts every time she sees a child.

Asti traveled from Missouri to Texas as a coming three-year-old. Fresh from a thirty-day wonder start under saddle, I bought her from a video. No horse can be three-gaited and work in a curb bit properly in thirty days. Asti didn't work from her hind end as she should, but her potential was evident in the video and I could fix the rest.

When she backed out of the transport in the foreign land of Texas, she never raised her head, called out for a friend, or seemed bothered in any way. She was immediately at home. Asti did, however, have a few issues. Every horse has issues. For that matter, I have issues and I expect you do, too. Her biggest problem was balance. Tall horses are like young men experiencing a growth spurt. They need a little more time and practice before they can organize their size and length efficiently.

The first time I put Asti in the round pen she took off at a canter, progressed to a gallop, broke into a full-out run—and I shut her down. I never asked her to do anything. Obviously, she was taught to get into the pen and exercise. Which, of course, wasn't what she was doing. She was out of control physically which leads to out-of-control emotionally. That's why I stopped her.

Instead of giving horses the time and guidance necessary to teach them to carry themselves properly, some people "balance" a horse with the bridle. The thirty-day wonder trainer shoved her onto her forehand, stuck a big bit in her mouth, and held her up with leveraged rein pressure. Without a crutch she couldn't keep herself upright. I never asked her to canter when longed in the arena, but if she did, she'd explode like a racehorse when the starting gate opens, hit the end of the line, and fall down with her hind legs splayed out like a water spider.

Which scared me to death! I was afraid she'd get up from the ground broken. Lame. Damaged. Thankfully, she never did, a testimony to how structurally sound she is.

Fixing Asti's balance took nearly a year. Without balance you can't do anything else softly, correctly, and enjoyably. Being out of balance is terrible, especially on the top of a horse. Imagine pairing a horse that can't balance itself with a rider who can't help. It's like the blind leading the blind except one of the two is huge.[17]

---

[17] Matthew 15:14

Balance issues complicate everything. I don't have an inner-gyro like most people because of an inner-ear disorder and TMJ (temporomandibular joint disorder.) The only way I know if my head is north and my feet south is by vision. I have to see which way is up to know it. I've been known to walk into walls, doorways, and even got bucked off my treadmill once.

I hoped to retrain my brain to bypass screwed up circuits by closing my eyes for a few seconds at a time while walking on my treadmill. While rehabbing after a knee replacement my treadmill and I became best friends. Hands hovering over the handles, I closed my eyes for a second or two and kept walking. I check my form in the full-length mirror on the garage wall opposite the treadmill. When I opened my eyes, I was listing to the right. I closed them again and walked a couple more steps. When I opened them I was leaning to the left.

The third time I must have waited too long to open my eyes. I didn't know I'd flown off the treadmill until I heard the sound of stressed plastic when I landed in front of the bumper of my husband's truck. Chalk it up to experience. I keep my eyes open now.

Balance isn't optional, it's essential. If you've just slipped on a wet floor or icy driveway, you don't think about your hair appointment, polishing your tall boots, morning spat with your husband, or anything else except landing with the least damage.

Few things are more distracting than being out of balance. Horses feel the same way. Whether you're contemplating physical balance, spiritual balance, or the balance in your checking account, deficiencies steal your focus, attention, and peace. Riding a horse requires multitasking for both horse and rider. Balance issues complicate everything. Do not underestimate the challenge. Whenever you're insecure, anxious, or trying to figure out why your horse isn't behaving—consider balance issues. Ask a knowledgeable horse professional for help.

Horse are spiritual beings in much the same way we are. Balance is just as important to them. Imagine walking around in one flip flop and one stiletto. Now, add a fifty-pound backpack. Climb stairs. Walk on uneven ground.

You won't do it, will you?

We expect horses to serve whether they're balanced or not. They can't pull off their shoes, pitch the load in the corner and schedule a massage. But you can do it for them. There are scads of online videos teaching horse owners to stretch, massage, and release tense places. It's a quiet, deep, immensely satisfying process for both of you.

Transitions often create imbalances, moving from season to season, job to job, heels to flats, day shift to graveyard hours, and ending relationships. Squeeze in time with others and time alone into your schedule —without electronics. Connect. Nourish. Find a new happy place. Saddle and bridle fit, feeding programs, exercise routines, hoof trimming, dental issues, and waking up on the wrong side of the stall all contribute to imbalances in horses. Never assume your horse is being difficult on purpose.

Feel his spirit. Touch him. Listen to him. He depends on you the same way you depend on him.

Reflection

Perhaps the mirror that reflects the horse and human works both ways, your horse reflects you and you reflect your horse. Your goal is for that reflection of horse and human to be a pleasant one, benefiting you both.

Horses often mirror the behaviors and emotions around them, serving as eerily accurate relationship barometers. Unlike people, horses don't lie to themselves or each other. The natural modes of communication for horses are body language and state of spirit. Many people don't realize what messages they send. Every time a human shows up a horse evaluates him or her as safe, dangerous, or of little consequence.

Watching someone tells you a lot about their behavior but little about their motivation. Horses watch what you do, drawing savvy conclusions about what inspired your actions. People are not as naturally gifted in this as horses. You can tell WHAT your horse is doing easily, but how often do you know WHY? Horses are more consistent than people because they're not confused about who they are, Who made them, and Who is in charge. Recently I received a little blow back on my opinion about the relative constancy of horses and humans.

"Lynn, I have to disagree with you that horses are more consistent than humans. My younger horse can be all over the map within split seconds. One minute he's charming, the next minute he's having a temper tantrum, then he gets scared, then he gets really bossy."

This horse sounds like lots of people I've met over the years. They're moody and reactive, changing in a flash based on what they had for lunch, who looked at them cross-ways, and if they're not getting what they think they want. Those folks are consistently inconsistent, just like their horses. Did it start with the horse, the owner, or did the owner pick a horse with a personality similar to her own?

Samantha Harvey, *Alternative Horsemanship*, contributed a comment to the discussion that deserves to be shared. I edited it for brevity and share it with her permission.

As a "reflection of us" example I think of a clinic offered to new students. They stood facing me in a semi-circle with their horses standing behind them held with just the lead rope. I was giving an overview asking nothing of the students.

One horse was agitated, busy, couldn't stand still. The horse next to him looked like he was bored. Without saying anything, I switched the busy horse's handler with the disinterested horse's handler.

Again, I was just talking, handlers holding horses with their backs to the horses asking nothing of them. Within five minutes of the switch, the busy horse blew his nose, passed manure, dropped his head, cocked a rear foot and dozed off. The other originally disinterested horse became more and more agitated.

It doesn't take much, and people are often unaware of the baggage they bring with them to the barn. I suggest folks leave reality at the door. Take time to get emotionally and mentally clear before you show up to work with your horse.

What do you think about the following observation? Does mirroring really differ from reacting? How? Can you say that being in a hurry doesn't impact your spirit? Cool, calm, and collected is a different vibe from rushed, rabid, and scattered.

"After all these years, I don't see horses mirroring my mood or intentions so much as reacting to my behavior. If I'm in a rush, the horses are more likely to be edgy, not because of my mood—which may be just dandy—but because I'm moving faster than their minds can accommodate and instinct kicks in." — unknown

The owner who knowingly pushes a horse "faster than their minds can accommodate" is asking for a negative response, like being edgy as noted in the previous comment. In my opinion, the horse absolutely reflects the spirit of the human.

What causes *rush*? It's possible to work more efficiently when time is limited, but I don't think of that as rush. The type of *rush* that affects horse is that which is disquieting to the spirit. Emergencies happen. If you need to involve your horse, put a lid on your own emotional turmoil, settle, and slow down. The change in you will be reflected by a similar change in your horse.

Students reflect the spirit, instruction, and personalities of not just the teacher, but parents, friends, and circumstances. Owners who board their horses away from home have to consider what happens when they aren't present.

Relationship is Unique and Personal

Every parent-child relationship is unique. Savvy parents develop rules and lessons to benefit each child. Coaches change exercises and motivation for individual development as well as team benefit. No one coaches or conditions a ninety-pound teen-age female gymnast the same way as a thirty-year-old NFL linebacker.

The needs of the child, athlete, or horse dictate the way leadership is applied by the worthy and effective parent, coach, and horse owner (trainer). Bold horses seek bold leadership. Horses who are fearful seek leadership that reassures as well as builds their confidence.

Here's another perspective, "If my horses mirrored me, I would have to be the seven faces of Eve because they are all different in how they act and react to the same situation and to me. I think people sometimes believe their horses and dogs are like them, but I think it's because animals adapt to their environment and how their handlers act."

God is the same yesterday, today, and forever[18] though the specifics of His leadership vary based on the needs of the person. Each one brings something different to the "family" just like the horses belonging to whoever wrote the previous comment.

---

[18] Hebrews 13:8, Psalm 102:26-27

The Breath of Horse Crazy

Jessica Shively

I was three years old when Grandpa visited my family in Idaho. He surprised me with a bay-colored Wonder Horse, a plastic horse with a rocking frame. I took that toy to a whole different level, passionately riding the horse, frame and all, around the house and yard.

I slept on that horse and ate breakfast, lunch and dinner on my Wonder pony. When I woke out of a dead sleep I cried because I wasn't done riding my Wonder horse. If Mom would have allowed it, I would've lived every minute on that plastic wonder horse.

From that moment, the breath of horse crazy was instilled in me.

Grandpa surprised me with a trip to JR Stables when I was six-years-old, somewhere in the middle of nowhere in central Illinois. The owner, Jeannie, took me under her wing and taught me so much. I took lessons and mucked stalls, anything and everything I could to stay in the barn.

Fast forward five or six years. Jeannie asked if I wanted to ride a more challenging horse named Rocket. Rocket was a two-year-old coming on three. He was, and still is, the most beautiful tobiano paint, with a dun line and mane and tail you would just drool over. Of course, I said yes. Rocket is one of those horses that make good riders. He taught me to sit deep in a buck, dismount fast for a roll, how to fix my seat in a jump, relax on a trail, master dirt skiing, and gave me his all once we worked out our miscommunications.

Rocket was there for me when I lost my mother just after turning sixteen. He was there when I enlisted in the Marine Corps and when I came back from deployment. Rocket was there when I lost my father and when I married my husband. Rocket knows all my secrets and soaked up buckets of tears. He's seen me at my worst and pushes me to be my best, the same as Christ does, as I grow in my faith.

A few years after we got married, my husband surprised me by bringing Rocket to our state. He now resides in my front pasture where I tuck him safely in each night and see him first thing every morning. Rocket recently turned nineteen-years-old. I pray every day, "Thank you Lord for the gifts you've given me. Thank you for my testimonies, my wonderful husband, and my handsome boy, Rocket."

I've learned so much from every experience, and I'm truly thankful for the wisdom the Lord provides, allowing me to see truth in every battle. Challenges makes you stronger and prepare you to be an overcomer and light in this world. Let His light shine through.

Jessica founded and serves her community through Trail of Faith Farms. We connected online, chat on the phone, and I'm thrilled to consider her part of my extended equine family. She exudes love, creativity, irresistible personality, and commitment. Jessica serves all horse enthusiasts, whether able-bodied or limited, and by doing that well, serves her precious Lord. Some women become equine professionals later in life, while others, like Jessica, jump in with both feet and start swimming.

The Tween-Ager

The tween-age youth exhibitor rode an attractive well-schooled horse. So far, they'd earned excellent marks in the large trail class I judged in gorgeous Helena, Montana. Her matching ivory blouse, slacks, microfiber chaps, and cowboy hat screamed *Equitation*. Equally put-together, her horse's tack was well-fitting, polished, and fashionable.

Impressed so far, I expected her to place well.

She approached the next obstacle, lightly shifted her weight, turned out one toe, barely lifted her rein hand and moved it one inch to the side. In response, her horse performed a perfect pivot on his haunches. A thing of beauty; balanced, clean, and cadenced. It would have earned the highest mark - except it wasn't the right move.

The tween-ager stopped, rudely banging her horse in the mouth with a heavy curb bit. Not satisfied with that abuse, she solidly bounced roweled spurs against his sides. The maneuver didn't go as planned and she was mad. At her horse.

The young lady blamed her horse for messing up the obstacle and ruining her chances for a win. I knew the horse did exactly as she asked. The error was hers. What she asked her horse was not what she intended.[19] As a result, she punished him for perfect obedience.

Three things about that trip remain with me to this day. One, the impression left by this tween-ager. Two, a

---

[19] Romans 7:15, 19

wonderful memory of judging with a gentleman I loved as a brother. Three, the amazing blueberry pancakes served in the hotel dining room. I ate them for breakfast every day and stashed extras in my room for snacking.

The next time I met with other judges for continuing education and re-certification I mentioned this rider in a session. Her behavior wasn't unique. I witnessed it too often and felt for the horse each time. Rules require judges to consider each trail obstacle separately, but I always added an overall impression score which often served as a tie-breaker.

The tween-ager got a zero in that department. Someone taught her to punish rather than correct her horse. Beyond that, it should never happen in the show pen. And further, beyond that, the horse did exactly as she asked. I later learned that the rules for judging trail changed. My fellow judge from the Helena, Montana, show said my input was a significant factor in new scoring methods. I don't know about that, but it's gratifying knowing the rules changed to reward excellence, not abuse.

For a while I wondered why the poor horse didn't dump the tween-ager and stomp on her. The answer is grace.[20] He took the blame for something she did. And then forgave her.

---

[20] Romans 5:20-21, Romans 5:8, Romans 11:6

Unable or Unwilling

Nine hundred pounds of horse screamed toward me, nose near the ground, feet flying six ways at once, his body violently arching, inverting, and arching again – bucking uncontrollably.

I expected the buck and planned to let him hump around the round pen, step in front when he came around, turn him the other way, and keep turning him every time he bucked until he decided it was too much work. But there's a drop-dead point where the game of chicken ends. When he reached it, I dove out of his way to keep from turning into a grease spot in the sand.

He never saw me.

The explosion continued another minute or so, body, stirrups, and legs flailing into and through rails until something told him he wasn't going to die. That's when I realized I faced a much bigger challenge than I expected. Usual training methods wouldn't work with this horse because someone had knocked normal clean out of him. He exploded into the unexpected bucking frenzy when I asked him to walk off in the outdoor arena fifteen minutes earlier, breaking away from me, dragging my longe line back to the barn. This was an unexpected twist because he'd worked well in the same place for weeks without a single hump or telegraphing that he knew what bucking was.

I couldn't let him get away twice, so I collected him up and walked him to the round pen. At least, that was the plan. It didn't work because the horse wasn't able to think. He was terrified, his emotions swirling somewhere in the endless cosmos.

The horse is Journey. Someone pushed this beautiful horse past his emotional limitations by repeatedly punishing him for failing to understand what they wanted; demanding what he couldn't give. When one type of punishment didn't work, they escalated to another, and another. They didn't break his body or his will; they broke his mind. My heart bled for him, knowing what someone had put him through in the name of *training*.

I'm familiar with equine panic attacks. This was as different from that as a pop gun is to a bundle of dynamite.

Horses and people come with a sense of self-preservation; when the going gets tough they're motivated to figure out how to save themselves. Journey went from mentally present to totally gone. Based on his response, my guess is they tripped him behind. When he bucked, they roped his hind feet and dropped him to the ground. It didn't fix the problem; it created a bigger one. And Journey went to the killer buyers.

Horses don't do what you want for one of two reasons; they can't, or they won't.

Journey wasn't unwilling to do as I asked, he was utterly unable. The trigger (I discovered) was the stock saddle I put on him for the first time that day. He worked in a dressage saddle for weeks, doing beautiful liberty work at all three gaits. Journey and I worked together at least six days a week with no buck. Not once. He was tight, shy, and protective of his hindquarters, issues that required weeks of positive experience to manage, proving that I could touch him anywhere without something bad happening.

Enforcement, or punishment, never fixes inability--
and no amount of education will fix unwillingness.

Inability

Inability comes in many forms. Communication
failure, physical limitation, fear, hunger, pain, anger,
imbalance, and discomfort of any kind promote inability.
Before teaching a horse anything you must supply his
basic needs. The bud of relationship opens when your
horse learns how much you care. Trust builds when he
learns that you provide for his safety and comfort without
asking for anything in return.[21]

Horses don't earn their food and shelter in my barn,
it's my responsibility and delight to provide it. Hungry
hurting children don't learn well and neither do horses.
It's hard to concentrate when your feet hurt or your belly
button is keeping company with your backbone.

Horses are better multi-taskers than jugglers, but you'll
get very little of your horse's attention if he's anxious or
uncomfortable. Horses are smart, understanding that you
failed to provide what they need for one of two reasons;
you either can't or you don't want to. Neither gets you any
points with a horse. Which then creates relationship
roadblocks. If you're not getting the response you expect
from your horse, figure out if the issue is inability or
unwillingness. The two biggest barriers to ability are poor
communication and fear. If the horse doesn't understand
what you want, he can't give it.

---

[21] Matthew 6:30-33

If your horse isn't able to do what you want, do whatever is necessary to help him by providing whatever support he needs. Rule out miscommunication and make sure he's comfortable. Horses can't always do today what they did yesterday. When muscles or wind are overtaxed give him time to recover. Maybe he has a hitch in his get-a-long today that will be rested by tomorrow.

Recently I took my first yoga class with a friend. It looked easy and didn't seem like we did that much, nothing but changing positions and holding them while intentionally breathing. Not too tough, right? After the first forty minutes I was winded, which shocked me. I'm pretty active, so why was this so difficult? Those of you up on your yoga are shaking your heads with pity; another amateur who didn't know. I learned my lesson. It's not all about comfy clothes. Yoga is for athletes.

The next day my hip muscles felt like the bands of a sling shot ready to shoot. My friend remarked on how limber this old gal was during class, but if she saw me the next day she wouldn't have been. If she wanted to help, she'd get me a heating pad! If some nasty rat forced me to do the class again that day, I'd have been a wee bit peeved.

Three days later I was fine.

If your horse isn't on her game, help her out. Begin by asking for something she can easily do.

Unwillingness

Years ago, an aging church lady asked my darling husband if he would dress up as a disciple for a Seder supper.

"No."

The lady was taken aback. Gentlemen rarely tell elderly church ladies no.

"Why not?"

"Because I don't want to."

End of story. Usually horses don't do as you ask because they can't, but there are times they just don't want to. When that's the case there's only one fix—motivation. The church lady had nothing important enough to offer my husband to turn his no into a yes. Unable to motivate, she had to move on to someone else's husband. If your horse isn't willing to do as you ask the only remedy is motivation. What can you offer that's important enough to change his mind? Every woman and horse has preferences, peeves, cravings, and deal-breakers, with her own idea of what's important and what isn't.

You could offer me ten new pairs of shoes hoping to get me to change an "I don't want to" into an "Okay." It wouldn't work because I'm not into shoes. But gingerbread might do the trick.

What motivates your horse? What does he want that he doesn't have? Sometimes the fix is simple. Lesson horses often burn out from mindlessly going 'round and 'round the arena. Offer a trail ride or go track cattle. Play games. Horses need vacations as much as you do.

Horses aren't the only ones who need incentives to show up for work Monday morning unless they love their job or love you.

Be Polite

Smart horses like to be involved in plans and decisions. Honestly, were the horses in your dreams dull and predictable or full of personality and attitude? The dream comes true when such a horse chooses to give you everything he has.

Asking politely always gets you further than demanding obedience.

General Silver was a smart horse; opinionated, talented, expressive, and willing to teach anyone humble enough to learn. General was one of my most important teachers as I was his. After a rocky beginning we came to an understanding when he was three, and I earned my 51% vote to his 49%.

A few years later a non-horsey friend and her more experienced friend stopped by my training facility to visit. I offered my friend a ride on General. The idea terrified her but she agreed to try. I introduced her to General and helped her into the saddle. I told her how to ask him to walk, lifting her hand up and forward a couple of inches.

"Lightly tap your legs and think walk."

"Are you sure you're ready?" General politely inquired.

She was. General walked off slowly and carefully, accepting the weight of responsibility for the outcome. They turned, stopped, and walked off a few more times. She asked him to take care of her and he accepted the role as her reliable trusty steed.

"Would you like to try a jog?" I asked.

Still a little nervous, she agreed to try. She tapped her legs on him and clucked, just as I instructed.

"Are you sure you're ready?" General asked.

She was. He lifted into the sweetest little jog, gently rocking side to side, dropping to a walk when his charge got the tiniest bit off center in the saddle. After righting herself she asked for a jog again.

"Are you sure?"

They both enjoyed a fabulous ride. My friend's confidence blossomed.

Then her friend asked if she could ride General. After seeing how delightful he was, who could resist?

"Sure."

She didn't bother introducing herself to General, but grabbed the reins, thrust her foot into the stirrup and popped into the saddle. After gathering the snaffle reins a bit too tightly, she prepared to give General her first command. He deliberately ratcheted his head and neck around to the left, looking her dead in the face. His expression spoke volumes, "Are you feeling lucky, Big Shot?"

It was a short ride. General expected people to be well-mannered and clearly communicated his position. Aren't horses curious? It's one reason I adore them. General would happily babysit, assuming full responsibility for the care and safety of an anxious rider who politely asked him to serve. He could easily do what the second woman asked but was 100% unwilling.

Because she demanded.

The Fix

When a horse (or anyone) doesn't do as requested, you have three basic options:

1. If unable, make him able.

2. If unwilling, provide motivation.

3. If you can't make him able or motivated, move on.

The hard part is knowing which is which, unable or unwilling. When in doubt, always go with unable. You'll be right more often than not.

There's one word that perfectly describes how I feel when I get after a horse when he couldn't do what I asked – but I asked anyway, wrongly interpreting "I can't" as "I won't."

Shame.

I ask my horses to trust me and every fiber of my being wants to be worthy of it. When you fail like I do, and you will, apologize, back off, and do those things that make both you and your horse remember why you love each other so much.

Authenticity

"What's your problem?"

Journey looked at me with an expression halfway between fear and rebellion. I asked him to come forward, so he'd be close enough to the water hydrant for a quick rinse. There was no slack in the lead rope, it was as tight as Journey could get it without pulling or coming closer. Nothing in his body language said, "Give me a second to get used to the idea, then I'll come."

I'm not sure which, but he was either saying, "I'm not feeling confident about this" or "Can you make me?" If I were laying odds, I'd lean toward the latter.

He was testing me. Again. Trying to see if he could goad me into doing what I promised I'd never do. Sure, there was a slight possibility he was scared. But it didn't matter because my response would be the same. Journey would come, there wouldn't be a fight, and we'd log one more example of *you'll please do as I ask because it's easy and won't hurt you.* Eventually the testing disappears, but there's no average time table. It happens when it happens. Offer your best to your horse and enjoy the process even if your smile is a bit forced now and then.

Whatever happened in Journey's first six years left huge emotional scars. After three years of the most patient work I've ever done with one horse, he was beginning to get solid. Riding. Ground work. Relationship.

Horses with history test their people more than others.

They have first-hand experience of the bad side of human behavior. I'm not sure it's possible to earn 100% of Journey's trust, but I'll settle for 99.7%. We're in the 95% vicinity now, which means his remaining fear shows up when least expected.

Do I get frustrated? Sure. Who wouldn't? The question is, do I react to the frustration? I'd like to say never, but no one is completely objective about themselves, including me. Registering any major emotion is counter-productive in most relationships. I don't do emotional. Probably because I've been a horse trainer a long time and specialized in stallions for years.

Stallions make you earn respect and require respect in return. It's who God made them to be. Treat a thirty-five-year-old Special-Forces operative like a preschooler and you're gonna have trouble. Stallions know a hundred ways to get you. Don't pick at them. Respect them. Give them a job and let them do it.

My horses are well behaved, secure, and willing. Yet several times a year I still hear myself saying, "You're not going to push me into breaking a promise."

Keeping promises is an integral function of integrity and commitment. There is no commitment if promises can be broken. When you're faced with deciding between easy and wrong and difficult and right—integrity looks at the problem and only sees one option. Wrong is never a choice. Right is always the chosen path regardless of the rocks and obstacles.

Three years later, Journey is at the end of the lead rope asking me to prove myself again. Not because it's fun or he wants to one-up me. He tests because he needs to. There's more work to do on our relationship. Success isn't measured in days, weeks, or years. With God and horses, success is measured by faith. Faith is the product of trials, obstacles, and hard work. As much as I wanted to pull on Journey to get him bathed and move on, giving in to that temptation would kill part of his faith in me.

Wisdom knows the right thing to do. Integrity does it.

Horses respond to what you do, not what you preach.[22] My horses don't care what books I've written about horses or the bronze trophies I earned in the business. They only care about who I am in relationship to them and if I'm trustworthy. Horses want to know if you make the right promises and keep them.

Journey's bath had to wait until I passed his test. Then he happily walked with me to the hydrant, another notch upward in faith.

Will he test me again? Of course. Every self-respecting horse tests people, that's the beauty of "What happens if" questions. In the early months Journey tested me several times a day. Now it's more like once a month, unless I haven't been spending enough time with him, making deposits into our relationship account.

The nickels and quarters you put into your piggybank as a kid maintained their value. If you had $8.96 and made no further deposits, you'd still have $8.96 no matter how long between deposits. Horses aren't coinage. They're emotional and spiritual creatures that need relationship. If you have a cushy balance in your relationship account and ignore your horse for a month, the balance will be far less than when you checked the last time. As your balance falls your influence evaporates. Other relationships move in to

---

[22] James 1:22, Galatians 5:22-23

fill the vacuum caused by your absence. Other people, horses, or animals take your place.

You become authentic when your words and actions match, emotions are genuine, and you prove trustworthy and reliable. Worthy leaders are authentic. A worthy leader's promise is as good as delivered the moment it's spoken. Authority is the result of experience, not rhetoric.

Bringing Ace Back

Journey isn't the first broken horse in my life. The last two sons of my beloved stallion, Sky, returned home in late 2009, nine years after we sold them as babies. Ace and Shiner were the princes of the pasture, beloved, secure, and bred for greatness.

Ace and his brother Shiner needed to be rescued. Their lives took an unexpected turn when they lost their family, their home, and their reason for living. God knew their circumstance and sent us to find them and bring them home. We weren't sent for any of Sky's foals, but specifically for Shiner (Signed by Sky) and Ace (Adios Cielo.)

You'll find their story in *He Came Looking for Me*. They came home with history, baggage, and issues. Shiner had panic attacks and Ace suffered from dissociative disorder. When he registered stress, his mind went to another planet.

Shiner and I slowly worked things out. He wasn't really dangerous, just clueless and scared to death of getting out of sight of Ace. Shiner is a week older than Ace and the two never spent a night apart as far as I know. Ace was Shiner's rock.

Ace is a tobacco-colored Appaloosa with a vivid red mane and tail. Of average height for a show horse, he has beautiful angles, gaits, and is flawless except for a bump on his face. Ace got the bump on his nose from some training gimmick or mechanism in the wrong hands. He was different. Fickle. Some of his reactions were extreme. When stressed, he ground his teeth, ran backwards, or reared.

It took a total knee replacement to make me confident enough in the saddle to address Ace's demons—and years to figure them out. I didn't get what I wanted from him because I didn't know how to ask. Ace didn't respond to normal training.

Ace was a tricky case, difficult to pigeonhole, the angle of his ears being the only tell in his body language between abject fear and attempting to get away with something. Wily and worried looked almost the same. When you can't tell whether a horse is unable to do as you ask or unwilling to do as you ask, the only appropriate response is giving him the benefit of your doubt. I had to assume Ace was unable. For whatever reason, he couldn't act or react normally.

Journey didn't mix messages like Ace. Journey was terrified. Ace was either afraid or just messing with me. Journey was easy to read. Ace had two fright faces, one real and one feigned.

Shiner balled up or refused to go forward, panicking without bolting or bucking. Ace could throw a bite, cow kick, and buck in five minutes of walk. Once my knee was replaced and I was riding again, I knew it was now or never for Ace; never not being a serious option.

Ace went into training, progressing well for a couple of weeks. I thought, *this isn't going to be nearly as tough as I expected.* Each day we warmed up inside before riding to the outdoor arena to walk and trot circles, working a variety of ground poles exercises, reinforcing the previous day's lesson while trying one small new thing.

Ace progressed so quickly that I decided to walk directly outside and get to work. I mounted in the arena and asked Ace to walk off. He seemed a little preoccupied, but nothing major. Maybe he got out of bed on the wrong side. I wasn't concerned, but five minutes after we began, Ace left the building to look for Elvis.

Until that moment, whenever I said "whoa", Ace parked it. Stiff-legged, hollowed back, head in the air, bundle of tense horse STOP. Every day I worked to reduce the mental and physical stress Ace associated with "whoa" by standing, petting, doing easy lateral yields, resting my hands leisurely back on his hips, waiting for a sigh signaling release.

Until Ace relaxed, I was prepared to wait for the change of seasons. I wanted Ace to ease into a stop instead of slamming on the brakes. I couldn't even think *whoa* without bringing him to an immediate standstill.

When Ace dissociates, he doesn't hear, feel, or respond —to anything. I said "whoa." Ace wasn't home. He walked around at a brisk pace, with no obvious reason for where he went. He didn't respond to any normal rein or leg cues. Every chain of communication was severed.

I didn't know what to do, fearing that anything I did BIG enough to pull Ace back to earth might seem like a saber-tooth tiger on his back. I didn't want to add that unknown to my already dicey situation. It took forty-five minutes of aimless pacing before I could get off safely. I took it.

Over the next few years I tried several programs, looking for something that moved Ace forward, hoping to win ground we could claim and keep.

I vividly remember the day Journey made his

commitment. It took eight years before Ace decided I was worthy of his trust.

It was worth the wait.

It always is.

Heart's Desire

Shirley Cook

As a young girl back in the 50s, I remember traveling every other weekend to my grandparent's country home, counting horses along the way so I could "stamp" every white horse I could find. What that meant was licking my thumb, placing it in the palm of my other hand, then lifting and slapping where my thumb was like putting a stamp on a letter.

I believed that if I stamped enough horses, one day my wish would come true and I'd get my own horse. The stamps worked, but it would be many years before I had a horse of my own.

During those visits, an old cowboy named Toss came to jaw with my blacksmith grandfather. While they talked, I spent hours standing on the side of Toss's horse trailer petting and conversing with Laddie, the seven-year-old bay Quarter Horse gelding with a beautiful white star waiting patiently inside. Poppy pounded out new horseshoes or repaired broken tractor parts while Toss waited, stretching each project to last as long the conversation warranted.

One day, Toss noticed my passion for horses and offered to unload his horse for me to ride. Fantasy turned into reality as I unloaded Laddie and mounted the first time. Toss trusting me with his working horse made me feel so important. It's a gift I still cherish today, as fresh and amazing as it was so many years ago. The joy and excitement riding Laddie fueled my love for horses and my heart's desire to have my very own. Toss showed up regularly and he let me ride Laddie back to the barn where I unsaddled, brushed, fed, and turned out my majestic trusted steed.

This was my happy place, pretending that Laddie was mine. It would be another forty years before I got the first horse I could call my own. For five years my husband Don and I looked for property close to his work. It seemed like having our own place wasn't in God's plan. Not long after we gave up our search, trying to make our dream come true, God provided a beautiful piece of land just thirty minutes from Don's office.

Less than two weeks after moving in a friend told us about a pregnant mare for sale. Molly was a gentle sorrel Quarter Horse who foaled a beautiful filly we named Fancy. My heart burst with joy. I felt like a real cowgirl because I owned not one, but two horses! A few years later I felt called to share the wonderful God-given gifts of our horses and little farm with others.

Over the past ten years at least 281 different women have fellowshipped here, sharing devotional lessons and riding our horses as part of Heart's Desire Ministry. The more I teach others about horses the more I learn myself. I'll never forget the blessing Toss gave me by sharing his partner, Laddie. Our horses bless other women in the same way, from those who never imagined they'd sit on a horse to a ninety-six-year-old horsewoman who hadn't sat in a saddle for decades.

From a little girl who stamped white horses to a grandmother who lives and serves with horses, I know that the dream never dies and it's never too late.

———

Shirley and I met the first year she offered her ministry to women when a series of events led to my speaking at a Heart's Desire meeting. Shirley's cousin, Jeannine, and I nearly ran into each other in the doorway of the largest equine emporium in our area. She'd just purchased two of my books and saw another stack in my arms. Jeannine introduced herself, establishing a beginning. I asked Shirley to share her story with you because she is an accomplished horsewoman in every way that matters, has a huge heart that serves as naturally as she breathes, and is now one of my dear friends. God continues to bless us both through horses.

If you aren't living your dream yet, don't give up, but don't force the timing if it isn't right. Keep your eyes and spirit sensitive to open doors. When the subject is horses, the possibilities are unlimited, and I encourage you to love them any way you can.

Have you tried "stamping" every white horse you see? It can't hurt. Ask Shirley.

"Delight yourself also in the Lord, And He shall give you the desires of your heart."

Psalm 37:4

Lynn Baber

Faith Over Fear

"That's the thing about faith. If you don't have it, you can't understand it. And if you do, no explanation is necessary."

Kira Nery

When the going gets *interesting* I want my horses to find security in me, with more confidence in my word than their own instincts. In times of trouble, I want to be their ocean of calm. Bold horses are secure in their abilities, your wisdom, and the strength of your partnership.

This is my dream, offering loving mastership to a horse and receiving his enthusiastic acceptance. Not because he has to, but because he wants to. More than maneuvers, skills, or fellowship, I want my horses to be confident in my ability, commitment to their welfare, and unconditional affection. Faith isn't abusive, horses rejoice in it. Horses are born cowards, looking for security. Safety, companionship, and boundaries come from the herd. Unless your horse has a herd, you're it.

Horses may act big, but that's all it is. Just like folks.

Horses learn to have faith in you in a series of small steps, each one delivering a positive result that feels good. You must do what you say, be who you say you are, keep it simple, and put your horse's interests above your own.

Faith is a process.

105

Reset Your Relationship

Can you approach and halter your horse? If you can't, don't try. Anytime your horse leaves you when you don't want her to, she learns that your power isn't strong enough to deserve her faith.

Is your horse allowed to turn her back to you in her stall? If so, is it whenever she wants or are there specific exceptions to the *face- or shoulder-first* rule? Whatever your rule, is it always 100% enforced? When you put on the halter, does she stand quietly with her nose tipped in your direction, her head lowered so you easily can buckle or knot the halter?

Faith is important because it's the foundation of security, confidence, and trust. Every time your horse fools you, dismisses you, or plays games to make you work harder to get something done, faith erodes. Horses don't place their trust in someone they can push around. Without faith, your horse dream cannot live.

Is there any part of your horse's body you can't handle? Can you pick up and hold your horse's feet? Will your horse pick up her own feet when you ask? If you can't touch your horse's feet, quit trying to touch her feet until you have a plan that changes failure into success.

Is it easy to clean your horse's ears? Check her teeth? Paste worm? Will she let you touch every part of her body without anxiety or tension? Shoulder? Wither? Neck? Barrel?

If you're ready to reset your relationship with your horse, begin with one thing. Pick one thing you know you can accomplish. It must be manageable because you're going to show your horse a whole 'nuther you. Which means you have to be different and stay different. You can't fool a horse, so don't even try.

Pick one thing—one new rule—then draw a line in the sand that you'll defend no matter what. If you're not sure what I mean, re-read the chapter on Commitment.

Get this right and you're on the path to building your horse's faith, earning her focus, deserving her obedience, and living your dream. Get it wrong and you've only dug a deeper hole.

"Fascination with horses predated every other single thing I knew. Before I was a mother, before I was a writer, before I knew the facts of life, before I was a schoolgirl, before I learned to read, I wanted a horse."

Jane Smiley

Depths of a Dream

A strange stillness dwells

in the eye of the horse

A composure that appears

to regard the world from

a measured distance...

It is a gaze from the depths of a dream...

Hans-Heinrich Isenbart

Lynn Baber

Other-Directed

"For a human to win, it is not necessary for a horse to lose. You should not have to take things away from a horse or break him in fragments in order to train him; rather you should add to the horse. The goal should be making, not breaking."

Cherry Hill

Horses don't care why you love them. All they care about is who you are in relationship to them and if you're trustworthy. Are you a predator, savior, resource, or a rock? Magical dreams of flowing manes and bodies moving as one rest on relationship and love, a vision that never considers a horse as a half-ton accessory or tool. If you only want a horse to see what it can do for you, maybe you'd be better off with a 1965 Mustang or 1968 VW beetle. They're stylish, quirky and rare, and no one will suffer because you always have to be the center of attention.

In the presence of any horse, ninety nine percent of the time my goal is to offer something. What can I do for the horse? The other one percent of the time I should have stayed home in bed. Things never work out the way I hope when I'm more concerned with what the horse can do for me than what I can do for the horse.

"How can I help?"

I got my beautiful blanketed Appaloosa gelding Journey, when my husband said, "Try to buy him" an hour before shipping to Mexico. When he came home from the vet clinic after quarantine, he was thin, flinchy, and in

111

desperate need of care.

From the first time we met, I offered whatever would help him recover, asking nothing in return but that he try. I challenged him to trust me. To let me earn it. I had no plan. My only concern was healing him. Restoring him physically, emotionally, and spiritually. Working with horses, children, and most anyone else on a meaningful level is service work.

"How can I help?"

"What can I do for you?"

"What do you need?"

My success with horses results from being other-directed; not thinking about what the horse might do for me, but what the horse needs from me.[23] Most parents have heard one of their kids complain, "I didn't ask to be born!" Neither did any horse. Most don't get a vote about where they live and with whom.

When things don't happen the way you hope or plan, the next order of business is change. Embracing the status quo means more of the same. The quickest way to change anything is to change yourself. If you want to keep things the same, be the same. If you want something to change, you must change first. Most plans involve others, whether it's God, people, horses, or other critters. You only have the power to change one. You. If you change, so will those around you. What's most important is why you want to change. If it's just a tactic to manipulate others, don't bother, because you won't like the result.

---

[23] Philippians 2:3, 1 Corinthians 10:24

Make changes to improve, to give more, and to understand more deeply. Do what blesses others. Successful relationships seek to maximize others and help them develop. The happiest people in the world are those who serve others; they're joyful and loved.

Since this book is primarily about working with horses, you probably want to improve something about that relationship. Getting a horse to change isn't that difficult. You change, he changes. The trick is getting the change you want. You can't offer meaningful motivation if you don't understand what's important to the one you hope to motivate. What motivates you to say yes to a request? Why should your horse offer a yes instead of a no?

Self-centered people are experts at messing up relationships and are usually lonely. The people you love to be around are generous, caring, observant, empathetic, and creative. They're never selfish, self-conscious, introverted, or rigid. Inexhaustible love is a characteristic of chosen relationships.

Obedience is a gift. Not a right.

Other-directed people seek the gift of obedience from their horse. Making a horse do what you want may satisfy for a moment, but the only foundation laid is rough and ugly. The principles I teach never threaten dominance; they promise a light yoke and easy burden. In return, the horse receives peace, security, affection, affiliation, and becomes more than a horse through right relationship with a committed, worthy master.[24]

Horses learn to obey reflexively by experience and

---

[24] Matthew 11:30

blossoming relationship. They don't have to think about whether to say "yes" to your request or cue because it's automatic. In the dance of transformative relationship, the leader leads and the horse follows seamlessly, going with the spiritual and physical flow.

God knows where we place our *Off-Limit* signs. He notes them, then builds a greater relationship foundation. That's the way I approach horses, never leaving a horse in its place of insecurity. I work to earn the horse's focus and trust.

Over the years I've discovered that most issues resolve themselves once a horse learns to believe my promises. If a horse's body language tells me, *"Don't go there because I'm afraid,"* I don't go there. Addressing the horse where it's most uncomfortable increases the fear. As the amount of faith the horse has in me increases, his fear is erased.[25]

Love is other-directed. Leadership is other-directed. Offering relationship to a horse is other-directed. There are two general goals when working with horses. You either want something *from* a horse or you offer something *to* a horse. It's about you or about the horse.

No horse is perfect in human terms and no horse is junk. There's something wonderful about every horse. Every kid. Every person. People of great character speak in positive terms. They concentrate on what's possible, not what isn't. Another simple rule of thumb regarding positivity is leaving things better than you found them. Whether that's the guest bathroom after a weekend visit at your in-laws or a chance meeting with a stranger you bumped into at Walmart. Speak positive things into the

---

[25] 2 Timothy 1:7, Deuteronomy 31:6, 1 John 4:18, Proverbs 29:25

world. Too many other people concentrate on what's wrong.

Do whatever you can to balance things out. Wash away criticism with a compliment. Horses are like kids. Like you. Like me. We love people who love us. Those who tell us how wonderful we are hold special places in our hearts as long as it's done honestly. When something needs improvement, they deliver the news in positive terms along with a helpful suggestion or two.

If you're not helping, don't speak. If your horse messes up, don't blame him. Stay positive and offer something beneficial, no matter how small.

A pat.

Time to soak in the problem.

Smaller steps.

Togetherness without expectation.

Build her up, don't tear her down.

Positivity is a critical skill for horse training success.

Make it about your horse and everyone wins.

"The one best precept—the golden rule—in dealing with a horse is never to approach him angrily."

Xenaphon (430BC–354 BC)

What's in It For Your Horse?

"First, if you're fighting, you've lost already. Second, there's no negotiating power in being right if it makes your horse wrong."

Anna Blake

Horses are fraidy-cats, hard-wired to run first and ask questions later. Why do horses mess with people? Why do they carry hundreds of pounds of tack and human without complaint? What's in it for them?

Show ribbons have no value to horses, neither do trophies, awards, or even earnings. Horses care about relationship, security, food, companionship, and sleep.

Does your horse seek you out? If so, why? If not, why not?

Horses don't have to-do lists the way we do. A horse's daily agenda looks something like this:

- Check feeder
- Grab a quick drink
- Nibble anything growing.
- Nap.
- Roll in the dirt before the mid-morning nap in the sun.
- Check feeder.

Horses don't have goals. Neither do dogs. Animals are

simple because nature is simple. Horses care about spirit, security, food, rest, play, and companionship. Horses are herd animals hard-wired by the Creator to seek relationship. Dogs care about food, sleep, play, fellowship, and will happily interrupt their travel to investigate an interesting sound or odor. Dogs are pack animals hard-wired by the Creator to seek relationship.

Horses and dogs will literally stop to smell the roses. How else will they know if the blooms are edible or if someone they know passed by recently? Sniffing the environment is the canine version of Facebook. Who's been here? What did they do? Who did they do it with? Which way did they go?

Horses and dogs are outstanding power-nappers and often share a soft shady spot with a friend. Horses and dogs are far better at relationships than people. Dogs are beloved for their loyalty. Dogs will remain faithful to an undeserving owner, put up with little kids painfully tugging at ears or tails, and show grace and forgiveness even when it is undeserved.

Horses and dogs know what's important. They aren't conflicted. Horses and dogs don't look at a half full water bucket and fret that half is gone. They look into the bucket of water when thirsty and take a drink. They trust that the necessities of life will be provided.[26]

What do you bring to the relationship with your horse? What's in it for her? It has to be something your horse values. What you think about it isn't all that important.

Focusing on self above all else results in self-

---

[26] Matthew 6:30-31

118

justification, self-aggrandizement, self-centeredness, and self-righteousness.

Who looks for a solution unless she has a problem, or seeks enlightenment until she realizes she's in darkness? Who seeks a physician until she realizes she's ill? You can't establish any relationship with a horse refusing to acknowledge your presence. You can't establish a transformative relationship with a horse unless it willingly focuses on you, just as you focus on the horse.

Horses that obey *most* things may not obey *every*thing. Some they enjoy and others they're willing to do because it doesn't cost them much to go along. But when the price goes up—effort, discomfort, confusion, etc.—they quit or refuse.

A horse that obeys 80% of the time refuses 20% of the time. Obedience is earned. If you're not willing to do what it takes to deserve more, gratefully accept the 80% and move on. That's realistic. Your horse has the final vote on what she is able and willing to do. You don't have veto power over your horse, but you can offer your horse a better deal if it's worth the effort, time, or cost to you.

No one can make you do something you don't want to. Life is a series of options. In most cases you choose the one that's most attractive. Sometimes, if you're honest, you choose the least worst. That's a situation I never want to give a horse, having to put up with something he considers negative because I haven't given him a better option.

Traditional horse training gives a horse an array of choices, teaching him which one makes his life easier. Sometimes there's an "or else" factor involved. Motivation determines what choice the horse makes. Motivation can be positive or negative. "Or else" is generally a negative motivator. I prefer to offer horses alternatives that are good, better, and wonderful.

Think of it like asking your jogging buddy if she wants to do one mile, two miles, or five miles today. Some days are one-mile days, others are five. Horses aren't any different. Some days they're *willing* to do a gymnastics course but feel more like pasture obstacles or a hack in the woods.

The best reason for a horse to do as you ask is because it was you who did the asking.[27] Your horse wants to please and share his time with you. Horses do what you ask because they like the result of saying 'yes' better than saying 'no.' The only two reasons your horse doesn't do what you ask is that he either can't, or he doesn't want to. Pretty simple stuff, really.

The same is true for you. No one can make you do anything unless they force you by restricting your options. You may not want to sit down when a stranger tells you to, but three strong men can make you sit down. When you say 'no' to someone, it's because you either can't do what they ask, or you don't want to.

Horses learn to deal with physical restrictions. Fences are the most common example. A horse may prefer to go to the neighbor's lush green pasture instead of staying at home in his paddock, but the fence physically prevents him from doing what he wants.

What about other restrictions?

The journey of any woman and horse is limited only by

---

[27] John 14:15, Hebrews 13:17

what she brings to the equation. Horses offer you more than you could ever be yourself, emotionally, physically, and spiritually. One reason I've stuck with horses for so long is that every day is new, and with every goal attained I recognize another beckoning. There's no limit to what is possible with a horse. The only way opportunity ends is if you quit. And that's okay! There's more to life than horses. I cringe at the thought, but it's true. One day I'll take my last ride and so will you.

An indisputable truth is the nature of change. It happens and you can't stop it. You're responsible for the state of affairs with your horse. Know why you're in it and make sure there's something in it for your horse.

————————

"What is it with women and horses? Why do so many of us love them so much? I think it may have something to do with both power and powerlessness. To ride a horse and have it do as you ask, despite the difference in brute strength, is to feel powerful. But no matter how brave the rider, that power can only be accessed by persuasion — and perhaps this is a particularly female gift."

Molly Watson

Tribulation

At twenty-one months old, Sky, my homebred blanketed bay stallion was a prodigy. He was gorgeous, smart, athletic, boasted an impressive pedigree—and he was mine. We bred his mother and I waited in the breezeway outside his mother's stall every night for a week until he finally showed up at 2 A.M.

The moment Sky stood up for the first time he earned the t-shirt reading, "I am special!" As a yearling colt he was Grand Champion Stallion of all ages in several states. Now it was time for Sky to become a saddle horse.

The day Sky first saw a saddle up close I rode him. The first time he ever had a bit in his mouth he learned to guide. In the first week, Sky learned to go, whoa, side pass, open gates, steer, walk, jog, and carry stuff. The sixth time I got on him we delivered Christmas presents to neighbors. Many horses now wear saddles and other training gear long before anyone mounts up, but that's not how I used to train. It was ridiculously easy, a trainer's dream. He made me look far better than I was at the time.

Until it came time to lope to the left.

Sky did everything I asked because it was easy for him to say yes. He didn't have to figure anything out. He was smarter than most folks. Every physical skill he needed so far was a piece of cake. Walk, trot, stop, pivot, side pass, and loping to the right.

Loping to the left was a different story. Sky resisted,

Lynn Baber

blocked me, even offering what I call humpty-bucks. Nothing major, but for him, this was real rebellion. Sky was great at everything he did, except bucking, because he considered it too much effort to do well. I don't ride bucking horses and seldom had the need to. I've ridden a few stud colts who offered to buck since then, but I had more skills in my toolbox to defuse the situation than I did when I started Sky. An inner ear disorder killed my natural balance. I've taken horses in training to get the buck out of them, but riding wasn't the way I did it. By the time I stepped up, the horses had no cause for concern.

At first, I couldn't figure out Sky's objection. What happened to my obedient, easy, make-me-look-good young stallion? Then I realized; loping to the left was hard for Sky. For a horse who eventually won World and National Championships doing sliding stops, perfect flying lead changes and effortless spins, the first speed bump my newbie saddle horse hit was left lead canter. Everything else I asked came easy to him. Not this.

Loping left was tribulation. It was hard and Sky didn't want to do it. He preferred the easy stuff, which was everything else, a choice that most of us understand. There must be a good reason to fight to achieve a goal and Sky couldn't see one. Forgetting the left lead wasn't an option for a future show horse. But then, it shouldn't be an option for any horse because it leaves an imbalance that only worsens over time and limits what the horse has to offer. As a rule, horses with good basic skills get better homes than horses with baggage.

Purpose requires lessons, and some will be more difficult than others. Natural gifts may carry you a long way, but eventually you'll run into something that doesn't come easily.

Sky mastered his left lead, although it was a learning

experience for both of us.[28] Working through the process of arranging his body to make left lead easier for him took time. Sky blocked me, stiffened his neck, screwed his tail around, and argued that one lead was sufficient, getting as creative in his objections as his naturally kind disposition permitted.

My goal is building enough relationship foundation and physical tools to make it easy for the horse to do as I ask. Nothing you ask should present a brick wall to your equine student. Progressive tiny steps are easy, each one small enough for the horse to master without resorting to rebellion.

I didn't have as many skills in 1992 as I have now. But they got Sky through his period of tribulation and on the road to becoming—at least in my mind—a legend. Sky's story is the last chapter in Book 1 of the Gospel Horse Series, *Amazing Grays, Amazing Grace*.

Tribulation forces us from where we are to where we need to be. The best trainers make the transition as easy as possible for the horse. Difficult tasks present the greatest opportunity to build stronger foundations and instill confidence – in both you and your horse.

Tribulation is real, but when approached properly, it's also a phenomenal opportunity. Overcoming challenges is work. How did you feel the last time you pulled a sopping wet saddle blanket off your horse's back? Satisfied? Frustrated? Content? As long as the lesson ended well, it was most likely a job well done.

Sweat is a fact of life, not a value judgment. Besides,

---

[28] Mark 10:27, John 16:33, Romans 5:1-4

who doesn't love the smell of horse sweat?

———————

"My big palomino gelding smells like honey, and dust and sweat and some kinda "Mom love me" musk. To me, all horses smell like heaven."

Unknown

Humility

In case you think World and National Champion horse trainers don't screw up—think again.

I waited for my last ride for many years. Decades of knee problems took their toll and predicted an end to riding. That changed when my right knee got a titanium upgrade. My riding career had new life!

During my first ride post-surgery I realized I had a problem. And it wasn't my dependable horse, Bo. Who needed the fix? Me.[29] I knew I needed help, but knowing and doing are two different critters. Horses are honest and forgiving. And even champion trainers need a coach now and then.

I rode with bad knees my entire career. One orthopedic surgeon looked at my X-rays and said, "What did you say you do?"

"Train horses. Including start them under saddle."

"You can't. That's impossible."

"And yet, I do."

I smiled.

Doc shook his head.

---

[29] Colossians 3:12, Proverbs 11:2

My worst knee traded old parts for new ones fifteen years later. Somehow, I compensated for weak and painful knees with tricks of balance. The worse my knees got, the more tricks I used, but without knowing it. After knee replacement I thought I'd be back to riding correctly. Just like that.

Not.

All the habits, bad and otherwise, were still there. In fact, I couldn't tell where my body parts were. My brain told me one thing, video showed another. My body lied to me. I spoke with a trainer friend to see if she had any tips for me. She said, *sit on a chair*. I did. That was easy.

"Now, sit square on your seat bones."

"I don't know where my seat bones are. I can't tell if they're square or not."

The only way I can sit square in a chair today is to look at my toes and make them even. If I sit back in a chair, I assume I sit squarely. She gave me a few ideas for rehab, and I scheduled a lesson with her. I needed someone to watch and correct me because my deceitful brain told me my legs and toes were in perfect position, the same on the right and left. Apparently, they weren't.

My husband video'd me riding. My left leg did what I asked it to, but the right had a whole different plan. Viewed from the left my posture was passably correct, but from the back my right side was lifeless, my hip dropped, leg dangling, and my foot a limp noodle at Bo's girth. At least now I understood the challenge, which is the first step to mastering it.

Bo hauled up with me to serve as my trusty lesson mount because nothing I did would bother him. At least I didn't think so. I don't care who you are, sometimes you screw up and have to say you're sorry.

I screwed up.

In honor of the dressage trainer I dug britches out of the closet and wore paddock boots with English spurs. I had no leg strength, so needed all the help I could get. I don't know what I expected, but it wasn't quite what we got. She put Bo and me through our paces. Bo is one of the original amazing grays, a stout gray quarter horse gelding; a bit over fifteen hands weighing in between twelve hundred seventy-five and thirteen hundred twenty-five pounds. I trust Bo completely and we understand each other. I've never lied to him and no one else had ever ridden him.

The instructor asked us for a power turn, quick collection, and another power turn across the middle of the dressage court. The warm up was fine. Bo could do everything I asked but he wasn't tuned up enough to offer it this day. Before long I was using too much leg and too much rein. Pulling and poking, trying to rev Bo up, back him down, then rev him up again in super short distances. He tried but wasn't responding quickly enough to get the job done.

I stopped and apologized. To Bo. I told the instructor I appreciated the coaching. I did. She'd given me several fabulous exercises I could take home to improve my brain-seat-leg connection. But I would stop asking Bo for something he couldn't do.

The instructor wasn't riding Bo. I was. That made it my responsibility.[30] If you take a lesson, participate in a clinic,

---

[30] Philippians 2:3, Proverbs 12:15, James 3:13

or ask someone for help with your horse remember, only one person has the lead rope or reins at a time. If it's you, you must put the horse first. Sometimes that means not doing what the instructor asks, even if it's me. I'll understand and thank you.

The next day at home I reviewed all the parts I asked Bo to do the day before. One at a time and slowly enough to communicate and execute. Bo hadn't been at training level for quite a while. Months certainly, and maybe even a few years.

Humility is a gift. It helps us realize when we're being unreasonable; when we ask more than someone is able to give. Bo could do the complicated maneuvers, but he wasn't capable of it that day with his level of conditioning and practice. My purpose for the lesson was my own rehabilitation. I didn't consider how that affected Bo until I realized how much work it was trying to get Bo to respond. He took the brunt of my inability and forgave me.[31]

Enter humility. It's not all about me and I'm not always right. Worse than that, sometimes I'm just plain wrong. One of the beautiful gifts horses offer is humility. They reveal our short-comings and love us until we learn to overcome them.

---

[31] Ephesians 4:32, Proverbs 28:13, Matthew 5:7

Ladies Horse Society ™

"Horses teach us to stretch our imagination and make decisions and choices we'd probably never make otherwise."

Randi Thompson

For some women, the dream of living with horses begins before there is conscious memory or with an event or moment when she suddenly knows that of all God's creatures, horses are special. A series of recurring childhood dreams fostered Randi Thompson's love of horses.

"In my dream there was a magic lasso on the ground that was all sparkly. I'd step into it and turn into a white mare. Then I'd play with the whole herd of horses. It might sound a little strange, but that's how it began. I know how a horse's tail feels to a horse because I was a horse."

Sundance was Randi's heart horse. He was The One. She sold magazines, seeds, Christmas cards, and babysat to earn the seventy-five dollars it took to buy him. The day he arrived, Sundance jumped down off the back of a truck with rack sides, and his legend began.

"He jumped off the truck, my father put a bridle on him—I didn't know what a bridle was—I got on Sundance, my father slapped him on the rump and off we went like a bolt of lightning. I don't know how far I made it before flying thirty feet before hitting the ground. That was my first riding experience.

Of course, I got hurt. But I had such a strong passion for horses that I got right back on once I recovered. Sundance was a Heinz 57 horse, a former barrel racer, and no one really knew what he was. But he took such good care of me. We did things other people couldn't imagine. Sundance was perfect, what you'd call a schoolmaster today. He would have been perfect right off the truck if my father didn't slap him on the rump."

Randi was seriously injured in horse accidents twice, suffering PTSD, convulsions when mounting, and detached retinas from her most recent injury. Horses always inspire her to reinvent herself; after her first major injury twenty years ago and again five years ago. "Both times I wasn't sure I could come back to the horse world, but I couldn't stay away. The spirit of the horse pulled me back again and again."

Horses inspired Randi to try again and release her extensive creativity. Not only as a trainer, instructor, competitor, and clinician, but as a marketing marvel and serial entrepreneur. In 2018 she served as a roving journalist and speaker at the World Equestrian Games.

A few years after her first big accident she learned how to turn on a computer and access the internet. She hasn't turned back since. Randi dug her heels into social media, figuring out how to connect on Facebook, winning awards for her business pages and marketing work.

In July 2018 she organized her first Facebook group, Ladies Horse Society, using an image of Annie Oakley riding side-saddle for her logo. She applied for a trademark and dove in. There aren't enough meeting places for women who love horses. The Society grew by a thousand members each month its first six months. Randi runs the group the same way she interacts with horses and horse women elsewhere, with rules, inclusivity, and lavish inspiration.

"What's most interesting is women sharing photos and videos of their horses looking at them. You know that look a horse gets when it sees its person – it's SO inspiring and makes my heart sing!"

Randi makes the point that the Ladies Horse Society isn't an ego thing, but a relationship thing. She promotes images and conversation, about horses and the women who love them.

She says, "Let your horse bring you where you want to go."

———————

Randi and I met nearly ten years ago in Louisville, Kentucky when we spoke at the first *Women in the Horse Industry Association* conference. You know how some folks just stand out from others? That's Randi, and I've been a fan ever since. Her horse resume is singular, her love of horses and women limitless, and her generosity to share unmatched.

I may be a pro, but I've picked up valuable little gems watching videos of Randi giving a lesson or reading what she shares. Another by-product of life with horses is the amazing women you'll meet along the way. Have you considered that maybe you're that special woman to someone else?

Vision

"I find the best way to love someone is not to change them, but instead, help them reveal the greatest version of themselves."

Steve Maraboli

For years I wondered if Ace would ever be safe enough to throw on a light dressage saddle and ride off without running a full pre-ride checklist; longing, yielding from the ground, and checking his mental weathervane. For eight years my guess would have been that it would never happen.

I was wrong.

But it took eight years.

I bred, trained, and showed Ace's champion sire, Sky, and rode his champion mother, Julie. Ace is bred to be someone special even if he never sees the inside of a show ring. He and his brother, Shiner, were rescued in 2009 for a purpose. God wastes nothing.

Except for the vision I had of who Ace could be, I might have given up on him.[32] I rode his grandmother, his father, his mother, and siblings. I knew who Ace could be.

What vision do you have for your horse? What's your dream? Regardless of your specific vision or dream, you

---

[32] Jeremiah 29:11, 1 Corinthians 2:9

can't take a proper first step unless you know which direction you're going. God doesn't expect us to read His mind and you can't expect your horse to read yours perfectly. Communication is a give and take, back-and-forth exercise.

Goals may have dozens or hundreds of preparatory steps. Creating the history and habit of success demands that each step is small enough to guarantee success without anger, aggression, or anxiety. Every time you're in the company of your horse you either teach him something new, reinforce a lesson already learned, or a little of both. Continued success and consistency depend upon practice, practice, practice. That means you must have a plan.

Work with vision and purpose. Neither should be erratic, unstable or unpredictable.

Draw your horse to you by sharing your dream. I mean tell him verbally and with great detail. Describe every hope, image, and bit of magic you want to share with him. Help him realize that he's capable of more than he thinks he is because you plan to offer more than he believes is possible. Show him your vision then proceed to live it.

Don't accept discouragement. It's tempting, especially when others think you're wasting your time. Sometimes it takes years to make your vision a reality. As long as you're making the tiniest bit of progress month to month or season to season, don't quit. Understand that forward is a direction, not a speed.

My heart swells with joy when I recognize the magnitude of Ace's transformation. If I'd quit, I'd never know how wonderful he is. I would have missed seeing the vision become real. Ace would also have missed it and his gift would have been wasted.

The wait was worth it. It was all worth it, and there's still more journey ahead for me and Ace. Sometimes making an old vision a reality releases new dreams and new visions.

The journey continues.

"Horses... compel us to develop alternative ways of reading one another and, in the process, give us an additional language we can use effectively in the world of our human relationships.

Horses bring out qualities that resonate with or attract women: sensuality, commitment, creativity, danger, power, nurturance, compassion, spirituality, acceptance, seasonal cycles and freedom.

When I think back over my own life with horses and talk to women who share the same sense of connection, what emerges is that our relationships with horses are taking us to new levels of personal confidence and power, teaching us compassion and acceptance, and showing us more natural ways to resolve problems in our daily lives.

Whatever is depleted or missing in us, a horse replaces."

Mary Midkiff

Baron's Hazey Shade

Margie Shoop

I was the youngest of four in a poor family. Dreaming of horses was my escape from the reality of life. God was my friend and I knew I could pray to him and take all my fears and hopes and dreams to him! My parents didn't really have time to listen because they were busy working and then tired and stressed over money and life's problems dealing with raising four kids in Lima, Ohio.

By the time I was two years old God put horses on my heart.

I was reading at a sixth-grade level while in the third grade just to get to all the horse books in our elementary school library. I drew horses; I dreamed of horses. I imagined myself galloping alongside the car as my dad drove us miles and miles to the small county church he preached at on Sundays.

I prayed to God for a horse I could ride anywhere and do anything with, but specifically a horse that would let me rub his ears. LOL, it still makes me laugh. I was blessed in dad's small country churches to have people in the congregation with horses that would let me come out and ride. But too many of the horses hated getting their ears clipped, so they didn't like them touched.

As an adult I rode horses for other people. Families had kids with horses, but the kids never rode them. So, I did. One day the owner of a mare I rode asked us to watch

139

the horses while they were away. Haze was born that weekend. So, my husband Jim and I can say we were there the day Haze was born. We knew his sire and his dam, and I got the privilege to name him, Baron's Hazey Shade (Haze.)

A year later he was for sale and we bought him.

I have to tell you a fun thing about Haze's name. When I was a kid, there was a TV show called *Alias Smith and Jones*—with Heyes and Curry as the main characters. Well, of course, that's where Haze comes to play in his name but we also had a beautiful red golden retriever and we named him Curry.

So, I brought Haze and Curry together in my life with our horse and our dog. Baron's Hazey Shade, the best little Morgan ever.

Haze loved being groomed and God in his infinite love for us honored that little girl's prayers for a horse that would let her ride him anywhere, do anything with and let her rub his ears. Haze was my trail horse, my dressage lesson horse, my friend, and by dropping his head to your feet and pushing his head into your legs, he demanded to be scratched deep into his ears.

Haze wasn't an easy horse because he was opinionated and stubborn. Oh my, so much like me. On trail rides, if he decided he wouldn't go a certain direction he'd stop and spin around. We had many trail time training sessions about trusting me enough to just do as I asked. I knew I couldn't force him but had to be strong and direct about what I expected, including the times he had to be backed the direction I wanted to go. Or he would spin away – but ended up realizing that when I got him to halt, he was still in the same place.

Once he backed as fast as he could into the exact woods he wanted to get away from and got us stuck between big tree branches. I had to raise my legs up around his neck to keep from catching my legs in it. I think about how I do that to God, resist, resist until I realize I haven't made any progress and then I have to let God lead me.

When I was out of work and wondering where God wanted me to be, I went to the barn just to be with Haze in the quiet, watching him graze and drink water and rub his head on me. It was calming and I could be quiet and let God speak to my spirit, knowing that God provided for me like He does the grass and water for Haze. That even for me, He had a plan. I learned to accept risk in the jobs I took from that point forward knowing God would take care of me.

I see today how God kept saving me with horses, giving me goals, health, art, bravery, independence, a sense of peace, love, and a true understanding of stewardship.

All the things you think you learn or get from your family I got from God through caring for and loving Haze. Haze, my rock, my touchstone, my gift from God. Haze loved me, forgave me, challenged me, and as he became damaged by seizures, Haze depended on me for safety, kindness, and understanding of his fears and anxiety.

I learned from him and knew I would never leave him and would be with him to the end.

Haze Developed Seizures

It's September 2011, and Jim and I just experienced our horse having a stroke and then seizure. Since few people have seen this happen or confuse it with bad colic

141

symptoms, I thought I'd explain what happened to Haze.

Haze is twenty-three and in good health for his age. We went trail riding six days before this happened. He was lightly lunged twice during the week.

Saturday came around and Jim brought him to the arena to lunge. While Jim stood chatting with a friend—no moving around just standing—Haze raised his head opened his eyes wide and lifted his left hind leg, slightly cocked. He seemed spooked but didn't stand on all four feet like he was about to run. His eyes fluttered extremely fast. And then he tried to ram himself into the wall.

Haze got on top of a bench and then climbed over a mounting block trying frantically to get away from whatever was going wrong in his brain. When Jim was able to unsnap the lunge line from the bridle Haze went to the middle of the arena and threw himself—he did not fall—threw himself to the ground and seized, rolled over a full roll and a half with stiffened legs.

He struggled to get up—staggering—fell against the arena wall again—fell back down on the ground on his side—legs spasming—then laid his head down for a second and didn't move. Jim thought he was dead.

Then Haze struggled to get back up, leaned against the arena wall, pooped, then started shaking, jerking his head, making violent movements with no control—a full seizure. He walked frantically, trotting at times, around the arena. He hit the walls, tripped over things along the edge, jump poles, fans, plywood planks. Haze was blind and seizing up and hyper sensitive to touch. He didn't know where he was or what was going on.

When I arrived, Haze could hear my voice and came

near—but trembled when I touched him, dashing away in this frantic walk/trot movement. I walked a few feet away from him, using my voice and word commands I knew he understood, *ho ho—walk on—good boy*, all sing song soft. I got close enough to grab the bridle but was afraid he'd jump over backwards to get away and do more harm.

Then Dr. Kerns arrived and walked with him till he could get him in a corner facing the wall. Haze finally (this entire episode has been going for an hour) gave in and allowed Dr. Kerns to get the lead over his neck. Jim helped get the bridle off and Dr. Kerns put on his halter.

Then Dr. Kerns talked to Haze, touching and rubbing him to give him a sense of being with someone so he could give him some medication. I can't recall the series of drugs, but it was about three different shots. He took his heart rate and it was in the 80s. Normal, he said, was in the 40s.

Haze was rigid. Every muscle in his body was hard as a rock. He placed his head on the edge of the stall door and breathed heavily into the wall itself. I didn't think he would make it. After the drugs settled in Dr. Kerns got Haze to back away from the wall. Haze was so stiff he could barely move his legs.

He was blind and scared, hyper sensitive to touch and totally dazed and confused. Thirty minutes later, two hours from the start of this episode, Haze was calm enough for Dr. Kerns to lead out of the arena and down to his own stall in another barn.

It was painful to watch knowing Haze couldn't see anything and was so scared and lost. I could touch him and hold his lead in the stall and comfort with my voice, but he couldn't see me. He would raise his head so high at any sound and his eyes would open so wide trying to see and figure out what was going on. As he kept trying to walk around the stall and figure out where he was, I kept one hand on his shoulder, and one held the lead and I walked circles with him. He ran into the walls, bumped his head, hit his shoulder on an apple toy we had hanging in there. He jumped at everything. Jim took out all the extra things from his stall.

Dr. Kerns gave Haze a tranquilizer to help him relax. I waited until he was calm then took off his halter and lead. We watched him walk around the stall, more comfortable being in his own familiar space.

After four emotional hours, Jim and I were exhausted. It felt like I'd been crying the whole time. We asked Dr. Kerns if we should put Haze down, but he said to give him time and see how he comes out of it. I worried about brain damage and permanent blindness. Dr. Kerns felt the blindness could go away by the next afternoon. We checked Haze's vision before we left and felt it was already coming back by 6 p.m.

It has now been over thirty-five hours since this happened, and Haze doesn't appear to have any after effects. We need to hand walk him for three days and no turnout before then. He is retired from riding permanently, but we may be able to lunge him in a couple of weeks.

Haze developed cataracts, but from that time on he was tense, anxious when we weren't there, but he completely trusted Jim and me. We loved him and worked with him every day; his stewards, his guide, and his safety. Five years later he had another seizure as big and as bad as the first, ramming himself into the stall walls and barred doors. I was devastated because we knew what this meant. I am crying now, recalling that week.

We called the vet and we were with him as Haze left

our lives in July 2016. On that sunny beautiful summer day, his head next to mine, I rubbed his neck and spoke soft loving words to him. And then peace; all anxiety gone. It was over. Haze will forever be a little gift from God. I learned more about God's love and the trust He put in Jim and me, allowing us to care for this wonderful creature.

Throughout his entire life, from birth to death, Haze showed that the most important thing is trust, building the relationship and keeping the conversation going with God the way I did with Haze. Even when we fight, it's best to forgive, to encourage, and to steward all God gives us. To be a voice for the voiceless, to be the strength for the weak, to care for the unlovable, to trust each other when we don't know what to expect next. Most importantly, to enjoy this life God gave us and see the beauty of His creation.

God's message is that he loves even me. He's there for me the way we were with Haze. God is with me every day and will be to the end and the new beginning.

He's prepared a place for even me.

Relationship between a horse and the special woman who loves him is priceless. With Margie and Haze, it blazes out from her photographs. Six months ago, I saw one of her photos, the bond between the two oddly tangible and glaringly personal, inspiring a new concept for the book I was writing and giving birth to "The Breath of Horse Crazy."

I contacted Margie, hoping to use that photo on the cover. Sadly, she didn't have the image in a printable format but there are many others that tell their story and I'm grateful she agreed to share part of it with you.

Life with horses is real. It's a mixture of spreading your arms to catch the sky on mountain peaks of joy and wallowing in sand dampened by tears. The greatest losses reveal the greatest loves. If you have the dream, please know that it isn't a fairy tale, but a blessing that stretches you every way humanly possible. And those who live it wouldn't trade it for anything.

First Love

My greatest passion and joy for as long as I can remember is horses. When I was ten years old, I washed dishes at my Grandma's sink when a teenage girl led a paint horse into the vacant lot across the street. A horse! Less than a block away. My first instinct was to run out the door to visit but Grandma caught me first. To her, horses were something to avoid, not seek. She made it clear that I wasn't going anywhere until the last dish was dry.

Ten seconds after I hung up the towel I ran across the street. I remember nothing more, except that I got to pet the horse and talk to his owner. It was a banner day. I remember the view from the kitchen window like it was yesterday.

Decades later I drove the fifteen miles into town from my training facility to run errands, passing a few horses standing in a pen without the slightest reaction. My heart didn't leap, and I wasn't even interested, much less mesmerized. They were just horses. When did that happen? For years I walked into the barns feeling special, blessed, and excited about grooming, tacking up, training, bathing, and cleaning stalls. Now it was my job. Operating a public training facility is not only a full-time job, it's an all-the-time job.

The only minutes I could call my own were off property. Hourly foal watch interrupted night time in the first months of the year—until I gave in and put cameras in the foaling stalls. That saved me from the hourly trek to the barns to check on mares who often teased me with feigned restlessness. Once satisfied that a baby wasn't about to appear, I followed the familiar path back to the house, reset the alarm, fell into bed and did it again an hour later.

Two dressage trainers worked on my place. I didn't train their client horses but was responsible for their health and well-being. If a trailer pulled in at 2 A.M. after a horse show I went out to receive the horses, visit with the trainer, look at legs for injury or stocking up, flanks for signs of dehydration, and tuck the horses into their waiting stalls with fluffed bedding and fresh buckets of water as a back up to the automatic waterers. The trainer got to go home, but I had to check the horses again an hour later and an hour after that. Were they drinking? Sleeping? Quiet, or showing symptoms of transport colic?

Sleep deprivation and repetitive days can suck the passion out of anyone.

Did you bring home a new baby after giving birth? A glorious and blessed event to be sure. The end of a long wait and maybe even an answer to prayer. You adore your little bundle of joy, but lack of sleep and the requirements of caring for a newborn can dull the delight. Sometimes you just do what you do, forgetting the thrill of the opportunity because you haven't had a good night's sleep for months.

The day my heart didn't pump joy at the sight of the pastured horses I knew I'd lost my first love. It happened gradually. The more horses I had on the property the more help I needed. Other people dumped into feeders the buckets I personally prepared for each horse, cleaned the stalls (except Sundays), brushed manes and tails, wrapped legs, tacked up for me, and handed me whatever horse was next on the day's schedule.

I was the trainer but not the mother. Most of the horses weren't mine and I wasn't the one they turned to for a hug. As my career grew my personal and intimate contact with horses declined. Except for breeding. I trained stallions to breed. If that isn't personal and intimate, I don't know what is. Stallions required more from me than the mares and geldings. Success with a stallion is 100% about the quality of relationship.

I missed combing tangled manes with my fingers. The closest I got was pulling, trimming, and banding manes before a show or clipping heads, legs, and sometimes entire bodies. Some of my best horse moments came late at night preparing for a show. Most of the horses were quiet and I was the only person in the barn. I sat under horses shaving legs or perched on a short step-ladder banding manes, chatting softly, or sharing the warm contented silence, the closest thing to magic I knew.

Horses do make dreams come true, but sometimes the dream gets out of focus. To my delight and joy, God blessed me with the one thing I always wanted and the one thing I can never master. Horses.

When we moved from Phoenix to Texas, I exchanged the public facility part of the horse industry for ranching. My husband retired from his business and joined me. We bred high end AQHA cutters and reiners, I took horses in training, we had a small cow-calf operation, raised and baled our own hay, and somehow lived through the experience. My husband and I designed and operated the two-hundred fifteen-acre ranch ourselves.

Joy returned, and my first love of horses rekindled. I was the one who delivered the buckets, groomed and smoothed tails, distributed daily hugs, and enjoyed the full spectrum of life with horses again. I lived my early days with horses again, but on a far bigger scale. Horses live in this barn and I live here with them. We live together.

It doesn't get any better than that.

Maybe you lost your first love somewhere along the way. It's a stage many go through, like the terrible twos or trying mid-teens with children. You persevere in the tough times because you love the ones you live with. Even when they're difficult, frustrating, or perplexing.[33]

If the opportunity to reconnect with horses comes along, take it. Feed your spirit and soul. The horses will benefit as much as you.

Horses. You love 'em or you don't.

I love them.

---

[33] 1 Corinthians 13:4-7, 1 Peter 4:8, Song of Solomon 8:7

A Day In The Life

Every day is perfect, which in no way implies that they all play out as expected. A typical day in a life spent with horses comes with decision points, one path leading to frustration, the other to joy. The important thing is choosing wisely.

September 9, 2017 was a normal uneventful day. Nothing big, nothing small. No tragedies or victories. Just life with horses. It was an interesting day, from my first steps outdoors until I finally enjoyed some quality time with each of the horses.

To begin with, Ace didn't want to come in from the pasture. (That NEVER happened before.) Since I wanted him in and wasn't going to ask twice, I set out for the pasture, but I didn't walk out empty-handed. I brought along a hackamore, because even if I had to walk out, I sure wasn't gonna walk back. Instead of escorting Mr. Ace to his breakfast we went to the arena.

He wasn't impressed or cooperative—at first. I fixed that and rode him in.

Shiner had a personality blip and delivered a sly little nip to Bo's ear when he tried to take a drink from their shared waterer. I had a meeting with Mr. Shiner and got that handled.

Bo's confidence as herd leader needed a shot of power so we went to the arena for some fun with cavaletti pole puzzles. At first Bo was dull. I applied a little motivation causing him to stand up on his hind legs and wave at the crowd a few times (also a first, and great hang time!) Finally, Bo got with the program and we had a whale of a good time. We indulged in a little bareback trail before riding back to the barn, picking up my whip and tools along the way.

What a star!

Then there was Journey. I introduced some precision work with side reins before riding. He needs more education and deeper foundations, but also needs to get TIRED on a regular basis. There's no worse combination than young, well-fed, and under-worked.

All in all, it was a great day

Unbreakable

Andie Andrews

How I—a non-riding, non-horse person—ended up with a horse at the age of fifty-two, is a long and roundabout story. Let's just say I wasn't dreaming of horses nor was I missing one until "it" happened: that first, impromptu lesson on the back of an eighteen-year-old Quarter Horse named Hook that hurled me into a brave, new world; one that made me feel like a giddy ten-year-old girl with the wind flying through her hair—even at the walk.

No kidding. I was Hooked. Within a month, Hook was mine, along with a handful of challenges particular to a veteran lesson horse that was savvier than most of the humans on his back. From day two (after the glee of Gotcha Day wore off), I realized I needed a great trainer to help us progress in a way that was meaningful and enjoyable for both of us. To paraphrase a famous Oscar speech: I wanted Hook to like me. I mean, really like me!

I found that trainer early on and set about learning to balance my seat, my grown-up responsibilities, and my teetering mind that insisted at every turn that I was hopelessly behind the curve when it came to horsemanship—that I'd never be as accomplished at riding, at groundwork, or at "relationship" as those who had discovered horses in their childhood or teens. My lack of experience didn't deter me from riding, but it did cause me to become easily frustrated and to second guess myself over and over again. As a result, Hook constantly struggled to believe that I had his back. It was no great surprise when he eventually offered a spectacular spin and bolt that left me bruised, breathless, and buried face-down in stone dust. The irony is that in literally spitting gravel, I discovered my true grit.

I resolved to mentally cowgirl up and check my ego at the barn door. I realized a fall wasn't a failure, the information Hook offered wasn't an indictment, and if I wasn't going to think and act like a fair and level-headed leader, I sure didn't deserve to be one.

Our partnership bloomed in direct proportion to my growing confidence and resolve to maintain an unemotional and positive focus—no matter what. Hook responded to this positive change in energy and self-talk with greater effort and trust. We had found our sweet spot, which to me is best described as a mutual willingness to learn, to relate, to keep it positive, and to try.

However, when my trainer unexpectedly moved on from my barn, I had no choice but to begin the search for someone Hook and I would adore even half as much. I enlisted the services of a renowned trainer from a certain school of natural horsemanship. I hoped to refine our groundwork and communication and to further enhance my relationship with Hook. Instead, I found myself unexpectedly belittled, reproached, and my spirit nearly broken by a running list of "professional opinions" and criticisms that increased in harshness with each lesson and catapulted me back to that dark place where I wondered what on earth I was doing with a horse in the first place.

I couldn't do anything right: My tack was all wrong, from the saddle to the bit to the reins. My energy was all wrong ("too much and too chaotic for Hook's personality-type"); my understanding of a horse's brain, language, and physiology was elementary (apparently I couldn't "read"

Hook at all because as a writer, I probably lack well developed social skills); my position in the saddle MUST be tipped forward and cumbersome to Hook given my conformation and lack of experience (though this person had yet to see me ride). Boy, she said with a shake of her head, are you ever lucky to have such a kind and forgiving horse! Yes, she really said that.

Pigeonholed as her typical midlife client, I guess I was an easy mark. I suppose I was expected to feel doubly blessed that she came along to rescue my horse and fix me by default. The sad thing was, I nearly drank the Kool-Aid. During our third lesson, I watched her mercilessly manipulate Hook with a stick-and-string to try to get him to back blindly and obediently through a dark, narrow gap created by a sliding arena door—which included an awkward step down into a deserted part of the barn. Hook looked at me with a big question mark in his eyes. My gut told me to abort the lesson, but my head said maybe the trainer was right; maybe I really didn't know my horse after all. Maybe it was only my imagination that he looked confused and scared and was waiting for his fair and fearless leader to show up. (By the way, I had spent the last two years teaching him not to get too close to those very doors!)

The trainer finally gave up after several minutes of Hook's refusals and nimble dodging of pressure applied with her trusty stick-and-string. She clucked her tongue and told me it wasn't that he wouldn't do it for her. It was that he couldn't. My horse lacked savvy and confidence. Naturally, that was my fault too.

Nope, I thought to myself, he knows he stands a good chance of getting banged up between those doors, losing his balance on the step down, or mauled by a mountain lion on the other side. He's all horse—and a really smart one, too. And by the way, I wouldn't let you back my butt through those doors either.

She abruptly ended the lesson and let me know she'd be charging me overtime. Meanwhile, Hook stared at me with the same question in his eyes: Where did my fair and fearless leader go? His sense of betrayal was palpable.

That's when I figuratively picked myself up from the stone dust once more, brushed the insults from my shoulders and the tears from my eyes, and said: Lady, you don't know jack about me. Or my horse. The truth is, you can't break either one of us. Oh, and P.S. ... you're fired.

It was a defining moment, having always felt "less than" as a later-in-life horsewoman. But this time, I knew down to my bones that I was actually the one who knew more—and better! Don't get me wrong. I humbly welcome corrections and coaching in order to emerge a stronger and more capable partner. But I think this "natural horsemanship" trainer liked to break things just for the sake of breaking them—or for the vainglory of reconstructing them to her liking. At the end of the day, there's nothing natural about degrading or demoralizing horses, the people who love them—or ourselves.

From that day forward, I vowed:

To show up for my horse every day, in leadership and love. To trust my instincts and to honor my horse's. To have confidence in what I know to be true, sensible, fair, and good. And to always remember horsemanship isn't about credentials, it's about credibility.

My horse believes in me. And that's the greatest accomplishment of all.

Adaptability

I want Journey to respond to light leg cues. Straight legs mean *go straight*. Offset legs, one slightly in front of the girth and one a bit behind, mean *curve to match*. I begin with light legs cues then quickly uptick to bouncing or banging. Which means, I pull my legs away from his body and let them slap back. No spur, no heel. The further my legs are away from his barrel, the more pronounced the cue. Or, the bigger bang I get for my effort.

That started working pretty well. After one lesson he responded to smaller cues. I thought I had a good thing going and that I discovered a lesson plan that worked. A few more days of reinforcing the change and we'd be where I wanted to be.

Silly me.

Horses aren't machines and don't read our rule books. I'm not a machine either and neither are you. I expected Journey's lessons to continue without a detour—until the next morning when I was painfully reminded that I don't have the physical ability I used to. My right knee was already replaced and the left is missing a whole bunch of parts. Banging my legs on the side of a horse isn't a brilliant choice.

Effective for training, but stupid for me. Ouch!

It was time to stop doing what I used to and come up with something new. I have to find another way to make the point, letting Journey know what I want in a way that makes it easy for him. My goal is effective communication Using my legs to inform Journey's specific body parts is the most direct path. It's a great plan and might work for him as it has with others, but it won't work for me.

Adaptability is recognizing a flaw in the present plan and tweaking something. I'm tweaking.

"That's weird."

A year after a total knee replacement, my usual first ride of the day was on my BALIMO chair. It's like a wobbly piano stool that challenges your balance and core muscles. BALIMO stands for Balance in Motion.

The BALIMO made it possible to reset nerves that became too independent and creative. Running through a few basic exercises tests the range of motion in my back and hips. My routine begins with tilting the seat to its limit in the four basic clock positions; 3 o'clock, 6, 9, and 12. On this day, all was fine.

I felt great and looked forward to riding one or two horses. Like most days, I fully expected the brief exercises to go easily. After gently visiting the four clock positions, the routine involves swiveling in quadrants. This morning I was surprised when I couldn't get anywhere near the quadrant from 3 o'clock to 6; from my right side to the middle of my back. No pain. No stiffness. No issues, and no access to one-quarter of my normal range of motion.

I slept great the night before. The new knee was fine and I wasn't limping. There was no warning and nothing was wrong. I was stumped, *why couldn't I use my right hip?*

There was no particular reason. It just was. No more,

no less.

The only change necessary was limiting what I asked the horses that day. If I can't access one-quarter of my range of motion, I can't expect a horse to properly respond to seat or balance cues. Adaptability means doing what make the most sense. Sometimes that changes by the day, especially for women of a certain age.

Have you ever wondered why your horse isn't as responsive today as he was yesterday? Two things play a role:

1. You may not have the physical ability you had yesterday, or

2. Your horse may not have the physical ability he had yesterday.

Or maybe both. Horses are physical beings like we are. Your horse may not be lame, he may be happy, bright, and eager to work, but have difficulty with a maneuver you aced yesterday. You can ask. You can experiment. But you may not punish. You may not hold it against your horse. I was perfectly willing to have full range of motion, but it just wasn't there. Getting on my case about it wouldn't help, but only make me wonder what was wrong with whoever was bugging me about it.

Give your horse the benefit of your doubt. Adapt. Never sacrifice the quality of your time together trying to prove a point or master something when it's just not the right day. Try again tomorrow. My range of motion was back the next day. No treatment and no lingering problem, all I did was adjust my expectations for one day.

Worthy leaders have a back-up plan and are prepared for contingencies. Be proactive, controlling events, not letting circumstances control you. Bloom in challenging times, don't wilt under pressure. Be adaptable and flexible. Don't freeze up when confronted with unexpected changes in conditions or plans.

Make every day a good day. Live your dream.

Puffles

"I was always horse mad. My first ever love affair was with Puffles. He was a tiny little Shetland pony who lived in the field at the bottom of the garden. He was pure evil. He would ransack your pockets to find carrots and sugar lumps and if you failed to bring any, he would just rip your jacket open in annoyance.

But I loved him, doted on him. I have ancient curled photographs of 'Lucy on Puffles aged two' in an album my mother gave me.

After Puffles—and, believe me, I never thought they'd be an 'after Puffles'—there was Monty."

Lucy Cavendish

Equine journalist, writer,

psychotherapist and counselor

The Tools

The gorgeous dark dapple-gray gelding in the cross-ties came with a great pedigree, in both bloodlines and training. The owner paid a lot of money for him because he came guaranteed as sound, sane, well-trained, and open to communicating with people. The program he came from is well known and Rocky graduated with honors.

However, relationship is fluid, and even more so with a horse.

According to Rocky's new owner, he was spooky in the arena and intimidated her. In the weeks since sixty-seven-year-old Nancy brought him home he'd regressed. Rocky wasn't the same horse he was at the beginning.

Rocky lived in a five-stall boarding barn. Knowing I was coming to the area for a ministry event Nancy asked me to work with Rocky hoping I could figure out his problem. While Nancy was off helping a friend tack up I went over to meet Rocky.

I introduced myself.

Rocky was shocked. His eyes focused directly on mine, "You know I'm in here!"

"Sure, I know you're in there. Pleased to meet you. Tell me what's happening."

Obviously, no one here spoke to Rocky. He was used to relationship, being partners, carrying his share of the weight and expected to be included. Since he'd arrived at

Nancy's no one spoke to him; they only spoke about him. The problem was a lack of awareness, respect, and communication. The situation worsened as frustration mounted, in both Nancy and Rocky. She expected a robot horse, calm in every situation. Of course, there's no such animal as a robot horse. Robots are machines, not living emotional creatures.

When Rocky moved into Nancy's barn, he entered a relationship vacuum. He tried to communicate but never got a response. He quit seeking relationship and did his best to get by based on how he read each situation. When a horse is anxious, he looks for help, for answers, for guidance. When he doesn't get it his anxiety level increases. That's how God made him and why horses survived in the wild for thousands of years.

Relationship problems with horses are usually the result of communication snafus or the inability to diagnose a problem and provide the correct solution. Love provides motivation but not the how or steps to get from where you are to where you want to go.

Rocky and I had a chat, then went to the spooky arena to ride. We dialogued for twenty minutes without incident, anxiety, or refusal. Rocky was fabulous!

To her credit, Nancy understood the problem when I told her. Forty-five minutes later Rocky did everything for her he did for me. Nancy got it. The relief and joy in Rocky's movement and expression was priceless. He and Nancy were on track to realize her dream. Nancy was skilled and committed, she just needed a few more tools.

Obstacles

I LOVE obstacles. Whether ground poles, creative arrangements of sand-filled tires, or pool noodles waving in the wind—obstacles make life more interesting for riders and horses. Small obstacles also interrupt a horse's forward motion and concentration.

Ace returned home after nine years away with a fast brain; walking wasn't his thing. His rapid thoughts transferred to his body. Getting him to relax, think, and reason was almost impossible. If he was moving, he was going somewhere. The most difficult thing I taught Ace was how to walk on a longe line. Over time, his natural idle reset from frantic to soft and slow. Resetting a horse's idle makes training easier on everyone.

I first introduced Ace to obstacles before I had much control over his speed or brain. Arranging two ground poles in the center of the long sides of the arena, about twenty feet off each rail, I rode Ace in a line directly toward the center of the first pole. Just before reaching it I asked him to stop. Admittedly, the first stop was kinda ugly. Two hooves made it over the pole before he stopped forward movement.

Ace signaled that he didn't want to wait patiently, so I asked him to walk on before he did it on his own. It's better to say, "Please do" than "Stop!" It's better to stop a horse doing what you want than have to get him going again when he stops because he wanted to. You control your horse's feet, he doesn't get to control yours. Time your cues so you inform the horse, not the other way around.

After rounding the end of the arena Ace and I walked to the second pole. I asked him to stop before getting to it. This time he stopped without leaking over the pole. Again, we waited only a few seconds before I asked him to continue, because Ace got nervous when he stood still. I want his Go and Stop to be on my time, not his, so made sure I moved *him* before he moved *me*.

Ace is a quick study and figured out that he was supposed to stop right before he got to the ground pole—and did. *Good boy*! The amount of time he was content to wait gradually lengthened from a few seconds to several minutes.

Most horses don't head for the hills because they want to get there, but because they're nervous or insecure. Sometimes they go faster because they're out of balance. It's easier to stay upright going fast than slow. If your horse is chargey or too fast, rule out inability before assuming unwillingness. The odds are he can't do what you're asking the way you want him to.

Once Ace understood the pattern, we repeated the process at a trot. Instead of heading lickety-split to the end of the arena Ace stopped at the ground pole. The first time he relaxed and let out a huge sigh I knew he was open to change.

Ace stood calmly, no longer thinking way out ahead because he anticipated the stop. Obstacles create natural mental barriers. Instead of pulling on the reins, riding endless circles, or using other tricks to get Ace to slow down, it took two ground poles and twenty minutes. No sweat. No drama.

From there it's an easy transition to head to the open

pasture and repeat the pattern with our permanent obstacles.

"Trot to the next obstacle."

"Stop. Wait."

"Walk over, around, or up."

"Trot to the next obstacle."

I didn't have to pull on Ace's face because he knew the drill. His mind quit flying into the next county. He focused, considered, and stopped before attempting the obstacle.

Smart horses learn how an exercise works, then anticipate and do what they think they're supposed to do, resisting new information. Obstacles are amazing tools as long as your horse has to pay attention to you to successfully go over, around, or through it. Once a horse learns the pattern, he may tell you you're wrong when you ask for something new. Before that happens, mix it up. We trotted over obstacles or ground poles a few times; the next time we stopped. The new habit I want is properly placed focus. On me, not the pole or anything else.

"Ace, pay attention. I'll let you know when we should stop, go, or whatever. I got this."

He did. I love obstacles.

Let Your Horse Try

My one rule for teaching horses to enjoy obstacles is to LET THEM TRY. Correcting an effort in progress destroys confidence. Allow your horse to commit to a mistake before correcting it. Jumping in before the mistake is complete can create a crutch your horse learns to lean on. Don't use correction to introduce or teach, but to make perfect.

I consider the terms *correction* and *refinement* synonymous.

Introducing obstacles are "what happens if" questions. Ask your horse to try something and see what he does. His response helps you formulate your next question. Obstacles require a horse's focus. Getting banged in the mouth or stuck by an errant spur while he's trying to get over a pole or climb a tire distracts him from learning how to manage the challenge. Begin small. Build your horse's confidence.

LET HIM TRY.

The purpose of obstacles is to transform hope into faith. Hope alone cannot withstand the trials of the world without first being transformed into faith. People who place their hope in the wrong things or wrong people are often crushed by the obstacles that roll or fall into their lives.

Obstacles appear for one of two reasons, (1) to teach you to overcome, or (2) to redirect your feet (or brain.)[34] The greatest challenge on our place is Tire Mountain. Horses and riders reach the summit of Tire Mountain once smaller obstacles become nothing more than stepping stones. As a first step, it would be too daunting for most, and failing to meet its challenge would destroy rather than increase faith.

---

[34] James 1:2-4, Isaiah 57:14, Romans 8:18, Proverbs 3:5-6

God never asks us to do anything without first preparing us. He makes us able. The only way we learn the power of faith is to apply it. Horses can only be as bold as their masters. God is Almighty. Horses with faith in a worthy leader run to their master when tribulation appears. The true state of relationship is revealed in crisis, not in ease.

Stressed to Blessed

Some days my horses wonder why they have to keep learning. "Aren't I good enough as I am? I'm willing to do what you want when you ask."

Education always has a cost and there's truth to the term growing pains. My horses have it pretty good. Some days they have to stand patiently until I'm ready to untie them and begin their lesson, which isn't hard labor.

Do my horses sweat? Not enough! I'm sure they think they do, but working, growing, and spending time together is the reward of progressive relationship. Exerting oneself enough to sweat is good for the body and the ego. Many women have created amazing bonds with horses through mutual perspiration.

Maybe God thinks you need a few wet-saddle blanket days. Or, if you find yourself standing tied for what seems an excessive amount of time—God has a plan. You are blessed to be in His barn. I know I am. Obstacles and all.

Lynn Baber

Reward Every Try

Bear is a fancy little dun quarter horse gelding, built like a tank, the color of shiny nutmeg with flashy accessories, a wide blaze, four high white stockings, and a long silky mane and tail. Bear doesn't have an overdrive, but his transmission lets him drag pretty much anything you can catch on the end of a rope and dally to the saddle horn. If a rope can hold it, Bear can pull it.

Bear was a rope horse before we bought him, never introduced to the concept of leads, and didn't have much *whoa*. When we met him, his owner showed us Bear's skills and admitted that he was hard to stop. After a few minutes riding I asked him to stop. Ten feet later he did. I put the slightest pressure on the reins and thought *backward*. Within three seconds Bear shifted his weight to the rear. He only moved one foot—which was plenty! I released the reins and petted him. "Good boy."

I repeated the exercise for a minute or two and rode off again. Within five minutes Bear was softer and stopped with just the word—*whoa*. We took him home. I rewarded Bear for the slightest try. He responded by offering more. When it comes to training horses, less is always more.

What's the most important part of your day? I think it's just showing up, getting out of bed, putting on your duds, and stepping into what's possible, even if it looks like a carbon copy of the day before. Someone said that success is 80% showing up and the rest is details. In many ways that someone is right.

Face it, you can't relate to someone who isn't there. No show, no game.

Think of someone you love to see. Your dearest friend, your spouse, your beloved canine kid, the sweet elderly lady at church who exudes the love of Jesus, or your precious seven-year-old granddaughter. Just the thought puts a smile on your face. With special relationships there never seems to be enough time to visit. You always leave wanting more.

Now think of someone you dread seeing. The landlord on rent day. The convenience store cashier who wants to chat for hours when you need to get in and get out quickly. Your cousin-in-law Sylvia who gossips about everyone. The police officer pulling you over for driving with a bit too much enthusiasm. Your "friend" Gayle who can't talk about anything other than her latest purchase and how much it cost.

Do you want your horse to think of you as his dearest friend and most trusted partner, or as the law? Unless the relationship you offer your horse is attractive, he deserves a huge reward for not dumping you and heading for friendlier places.

I want my horses's spirits to rejoice when they see me coming. I don't want them turning away thinking, "Maybe she won't notice me." I want them thinking, "Woohoo, she's here!" My horses don't look forward to seeing me just because I feed them, but because I entertain, protect, challenge, and love them. And I make it easy—usually. I won't tell you that we don't have difficult, frustrating, or disappointing days, because we do. But they're infrequent and they're always my fault.

Yep, my fault. Horses are honest. In some ways they're as predictable as computers. Garbage in, garbage out. Punch the wrong key or give the wrong command to a computer and it will crash or blow up.

Q found stepping cleanly over ground poles difficult, most challenged by his left hind. After nine months of rehab he was back under saddle but not yet as stable as I hoped. God blessed Texas with a ridiculous amount of rain so we couldn't ride anywhere but my small indoor pen; out one gate, under a roof overhang, and back inside through the other gate.

I reward Q for showing up, paying attention, and attempting to cross the ground poles. Success with horses happens when you stack up one *thank you* on top of another. When Q finally walked over a single ground pole without ticking it, I treated him like a World Champion.

Riding straight lines in confined spaces where there's always a corner not far away requires high levels of discipline for horse and rider. When Q worked straight without any micro-managing from me, I rewarded him again. Whenever I felt his attention come into the saddle, I let him know how much I appreciated it.

Life is the product of your daily, weekly, and instant decisions. Great accomplishments stand on a firm foundation built one brick at a time. You always get more of what you reward.

Your horse does whatever works better for her than doing something else. This is true for children, teens, husbands, and horses. Reward every positive thing your horse does. Maybe it's only an extra scratch and "good girl!", a vigorous grooming session, or a drop of her favorite essential oil. Sharing three minutes of quiet time in the middle of a productive lesson is a super reward and sets the stage for a big finish.

Your goal is to identify and reward desired behaviors because that way you get more of what you want. If your horse isn't doing what earns your praise, you're not asking the right questions. Horses who earn the most rewards have the best trainers.

Do you reward your horse for showing up? Acknowledging your presence? Making eye contact? Nothing happens until your horse is aware of you and cares. Focus and attention are gifts. Be grateful for them. Every time. Some people are shocked by the power of common courtesies shown to horses. How do you feel if you make eye contact with someone you know but they ignore you?

Your horse probably feels the same way.

Have you ever said "hi" to someone without as much as a tiny grin or head nod in response? Being blown off is never the path to close relationship. *Please* and *Thank you* are just as powerful with horses as people. Maybe horses aren't impressed with the words themselves, but using them reminds you to ask and not demand, and to accept obedience gratefully, not because you're entitled.

Obedience is a gift, not a right. A try is a gift. Do you habitually smile while riding? It's powerful, encouraging, and relieves tension, especially when you feel insecure or distracted. Smile. Feel what it does to your core. To your seat.

It's amazing.

Smile and mean it. You can't be on the back of a horse without being grateful for something!

Small Things Matter

There's a box of treasures stashed away in my attic, things that aren't worth saving but that I can't part with. Silly things, like a lock of hair, ticket stubs to *Jesus Christ Superstar* from the original Broadway tour in 1972, a letter from a childhood friend I lost track of decades ago, figure skating medals from the 60s, a picture of me playing with the farm ponies who introduced me to *horse*, and a few other trinkets with no value except for the memories that live in them.

And a pair of heart-bar horse shoes. General, one of my special ones, was at the vet clinic when he had a catastrophic event and passed. I asked for his shoes, keeping them wrapped in tissue paper for thirteen years before mounting them in the concrete floor of our barn home.

When the small things of relationship aren't enough, nothing will ever be big enough to matter. Small things matter.

Boredom, time pressures, embarrassment, and inadequate motivation prevent people from enjoying contentment and daily blessings. No one is impressed when you nap under a shady oak tree with your horse. You'll never win a blue ribbon for riding bareback through the pasture woods. Cleaning hooves, stalls, paddocks, and tack are chores for some, but delights to women bitten with the horse-crazy bug.

I hate messy food, making it or eating it. Nothing is

worse than sticky fingers and icky fingernails in the kitchen. Yuck!

The barn is a different animal. I lost count of how many placentas I've picked up with my bare hands after welcoming another foal into the world, meticulously checking every tad and bit to insure it was all there. Cleaning sticky baby bottoms and flickery foal tails covered in nastiness during mama's foal heat isn't a problem for me. Crab legs, on the other hand, are too messy.

Am I crazy? I guess it depends on who you ask. Horse women understand. Breaking a newly tipped nail on the car handle is annoying but ripping it to shreds in the barn is a badge of honor. No problem—get it fixed, jet back to the barn, and carry on.

Everything Begins and Stays Small

Success is the process of taking one tiny step after another. When teaching, it's getting one right answer after another to little bitty questions. You make consistent progress with horses by taking a series of one teeny tiny itsy-bitsy step after another—consistently.

Like people, horses get overwhelmed. Some can take more than others before going ballistic or shutting down. Failure is often the result of overwhelm. Overwhelm is a leadership problem, whether it's losing control over your horse's reactions or your own.

Everything begins small. If you do every small step correctly, you'll never have to take any big ones and your horse will be the most amazing horse on the planet. People will notice and will offer you the moon to buy your horse or learn your secret.

Set up every request so the easiest response your horse can make is "Yes!" Like a string of pearls, add one yes to another, creating something magical one tiny step at a time. When your horse gives you a "No"—and he will—immediately ask something you're 100% certain will be a "Yes." Every knitter drops a stitch and every jeweler drops a bead. Pick yours up and get it on your strand. If your basics are in place, your horse won't notice.

The secret is staying small, correct, and as soft as possible. Keep it simple, hiding away precious memories in your trinket box.

Expect the unexpected. It's one thing that keeps me coming back to the barn every morning. I'll never master horses or anything about them. They're ethereal, spiritual, and help me become a better me. They know what I feel, seeking the rhythms of voice, gait, and energy exclusive to me.

Every day won't be the same. Horses have moods, physical irritations, and body rhythms like you do. Increased humidity can noticeably slow your horse's response. Some horses get up on the wrong side of the bed. Match your plans and expectations to the actual conditions of the day. You're not playing solitaire, but breathing the sweet air of horse-crazy.

Small things matter. Hugs. Scratches. Shared confidences. As every horsewoman knows, horses never tell your secrets.

Your horse's faith in you builds once you prove that you only ask for small incremental responses, rewarding each try with peace and affection. No dust and no drama.

Lynn Baber

Manure Meditations

Kathy Taylor

When I was five years old, I rode along to pick up a friend from her riding lesson and asked if I could ride, too. I don't know if I was aware of horses before that, but I fell madly in love with a little pinto pony mare named Jubilee. Is it any wonder that I still own a pinto mare?

Once I was hooked, there was no going back. Horses have always been a part of my life. They sure were easier to deal with than people, especially boys. I don't think I'm saying anything new when I say there's just something special about a horse. It's hard to put into words. It's their smell, the nickers, the times when they get spooked by their own farts. They are soft and regal; powerful, majestic, strong, gentle, fast, beautiful—all at the same time. I think we're drawn to them because they embody the qualities most women aspire to have.

I can remember the playground in elementary school, second grade at the latest, where my friends and I would pretend we were horses and canter and prance around. I was Glossy, a proud black stallion and my friend was Gold, a stunning palomino. We played horses all the time. My Madame Alexander dolls rode my Breyer horses. I didn't skip; I cantered.

When I was ten, my regular riding partner Pinstripe (Pinny), got very sick. A once-a-week rider, I didn't know enough to understand what it was, but it felt like I couldn't play with her for months. When she improved, the trainer let me walk her around and help care for her. Finally, she was ready to come slowly back into work. I remember feeling honored that I was the only one allowed to ride her. That meant my instructor trusted me to take good care of Pinny, no matter what!

The first horse I called *mine* was really a lease pony the summer I was fourteen. She was way too small for me at 14.2 hands, but she was my horse and I was her person for the summer. I still have the formal contract I made with my parents to clean the bathrooms twice a week in exchange. Her barn name was Ironface, which I thought was awful, promptly changing it to Sandy. She was a beautiful dark bay of indeterminate breeding. Sandy taught me that my emotions affect hers. If I was a mess when I rode, so was she. Who isn't a mess at fourteen? Horses are so forgiving.

I can't imagine life without horses, but never imagined how important they would become to me professionally. In 2009 I attended what seemed an interesting horse demonstration. I'd never heard of equine-assisted anything and was blown away by how quickly people gained insight into patterns of behavior that kept them stuck in ruts they didn't know were there. And, they didn't need to know anything about horses. I never wanted to be a trainer or riding instructor, and those were the only two careers I knew of involving horses. That demo opened my eyes to new possibilities.

Later that year I founded HerdWise, a company that uses horses to help leaders identify and close the gaps between the leader they are now and the one they want to be.

Lynn asked me if horses ever stopped being fun? Nah. I love the work involved with them—even cleaning the pasture. I call it my "manure meditations." They do, however, do double duty in terms of business and service. I only ride one of five right now, and when I was looking for horse number five, it was important to choose a horse who is friendly and able to serve my clients and be my partner.

Since my first introduction at age five, I can't imagine NOT having horses. They're part of who I am. I love that my horses are now part of my business, too, because they let me share my love for them and the wisdom they offer with others. If you think you might enjoy the equine-assisted world, get good training that focuses equally on both horse and human through the lens of relationship. Remember to always give the people and horses in your life the benefit of your doubt.

———

Kathy and I met right before her first HerdWise event when I received (and accepted) an invitation to observe. Over the past ten years, Kathy has blossomed as a horsewoman and credentialed professional, dedicated to helping clients think and live differently.

She's blessed me with visits from her two mighty-mini horses, Rooster and Gus. Though our calendars are usually packed, on delightful but rare occasions, Kathy and one of her amazing equines pop over to my barn to play.

Like many of you, I totally relate to Kathy's *manure meditations*. Nothing is as peaceful, productive, and more purely a service of love than horse-keeping duties. If you've ever held vigil with a colicking horse, you know that there's no more welcome sight than fresh horse apples ripe for the picking. One by-product of living your dream with horses is the profound change they create in you. Kathy's story, like that of other women you meet in this book, proves that success with horses isn't always a first career or even a second. Whatever your dream looks like, when there's a horse in the center, you're blessed.

Pick the Right Horse

Frito

Nothing is more exciting than shopping for a horse except shopping for your first horse. Claire wanted to save a wild horse, so bought one. I don't remember the details of how she found him, but she brought me an untrained six-year-old bay mustang gelding. He'd been out of the wild for over a year, responded well to a halter and lead rope, and maybe picked up his feet. Other than that, he'd never packed a saddle or rider.

Frito was already hers when I met them. She asked me to start him under saddle and get him solid enough for her to ride. Claire was not an experienced rider and needed a reliable partner. My first choice for her would NOT have been a wild horse, but this was her dream.

Frito wasn't my first mustang, but he was the most disappointing. Some mustangs make awesome saddle and show horses, but not all mustangs. Some wild horses are really good at being wild, especially the ones captured as adults. Twenty years ago, few trainers wanted to bother with mustangs, but I enjoyed working with a variety of horses, not just show stock. So, I worked with mustangs.

Saving a wild horse is a noble goal, but seldom the right choice for an inexperienced owner. Claire and Frito were not a match made in heaven. In fact, they weren't a match at all. Frito learned everything I taught him; to tack up without stress, walk, trot, canter, turn, stop, side-pass, and other basic skills.

183

He just didn't remember that he knew them from one day to the next. Every morning he looked at me like I was a complete stranger. I earned my first month's training fee the first weekend. Each day it took less time to remind him that he could be haltered, groomed, tacked, and ridden, but I had to run through each skill, in order, every day. Frito wanted to be a wild horse.

I told Claire that Frito wasn't the horse for her, but she was committed to saving this mustang and asked me to give him more time. Her commitment ended when he bucked her off in the round pen. She didn't believe me because she didn't want to give up on her dream. Thankfully, she was rational enough to know she had no choice but to let Frito move on.

Claire gifted Frito to a friend who was more than capable of dealing with his idiosyncrasies. After three tries we finally found the right horse for her, an older gelding who'd been down the trail enough times to show Claire the way.

Melody

With several young stallions in my barn, I wanted to test breed a variety of mares to see if the boys would produce any consistent traits in their foals. An own daughter of a legendary stallion became available and I jumped at the chance to buy and breed her.

She was gorgeous, the color of Coca Cola, with roan hairs throughout her coat, a stunning wide blaze and four high white stockings. Built like a tank, I hoped she'd produce a champion or two for me. Her sire was a champion racing, conformation, and show horse who produced the same. Melody had an awesome pedigree and excellent conformation. And she was flashy. What could possibly go wrong?

Blinded by the opportunity, I failed to check one other detail; her disposition. Melody was counterfeit; unreliable, nasty, deceitful, a Jekyll and Hyde kind of girl, changing from a cuddly pony to kicking pig in the blink of an eye. She'd lure you in — then nail you. She only got me once.

I managed to ride Melody a few times without incident, but she wasn't ready for prime time. I'd promised a fellow trainer in California that I'd send him a particular young horse to ride for a couple of months. I changed my mind on that one but didn't want to go back on my word, so I sent Melody home with him. She was safely in foal and I knew he wouldn't hurt her.

Sixty days later Melody returned. The trainer couldn't get her out of his trailer fast enough. She showed him her ugly side as well. We eventually came to a mutual understanding. She produced a colt and filly for me, but they weren't jaw-dropping awesome, so I sold her. Pedigree and looks aren't everything. The colt was a decent fellow, but the filly hinted that she'd inherited more from her mother than I wanted.

I don't remember who bought Melody, but I know that she went with all her cards on the table. She was sold one more time a year later to a gentleman who wanted a riding horse. He fell in love with Melody, loving her for herself. This was the PERFECT match. He even sent me a picture of his wedding. He rode Melody and his bride rode her gelding to and from the alter. Melody had goo-goo eyes for her man. She toted wedding balloons and does anything he asks with a joyful heart.

It's important that you find the right horse. It's equally important for a horse to find the right person. The best way to get a horse that can deliver what you want is to buy one who already has the goods and is willing to share.

When you're horse shopping, ride prospective horses doing whatever it is you want to do. If you're not a rider, then harness and drive, or mess around with liberty exercises. Whatever your dream is, begin with a horse who wants to share it.

The Power of Walk

"Trees that are slow to grow bear the best fruit."

Moliere

Soul rest isn't just for people. I want my horses to live there.[35] Bo is a great horse because his training happened over a period of years while we sold the big ranch, built another, and cared for elderly parents. Journey (I hope) will be the same—eventually.

Nervous or reactive horses often go too fast. One of my most popular articles continues to be, "How to Get Your Horse to Slow Down."

My first goal with a reactive or special-needs horse is to slow down his brain and reset his idle. Walk becomes his default on both the ground and mounted. It takes time and patience but is a necessary step. The quality of the horse's life depends on it. You already know how I reset Ace's idle. Horses who lightly shift into higher gears are delightful as long as they're just as good shifting down. Willing to embrace tranquility. Think. Process. Respond. Prepared to share your experiences together.

What's the state of your transmission? Could your idle use a tune-up?

It's possible that the majority of negative experiences

---

[35] Matthew 11:28

for both horse and rider are due to the failure to appreciate the value of the walk. How much trouble can you get into at the walk? Get the walk right and a host of other problems fix themselves.

Confidence and *Impatience* both like to ride fast, but *Confidence* enjoys walking as much as galloping. *Impatience* usually has a poor walk because it's unable to concentrate, harness undisciplined thoughts, or entertain the concept of precision. *Impatience* lusts for immediate gratification, not the joys and rhythms of building solid foundations and deep relationship.

Impatience plays the field and eventually ends up alone or paying for companionship. *Impatience* always has to catch its horse, because horses would just as soon pass on the chance to partner up. *Impatience* only seeks its own desire. It isn't a team player.

The best horse trainers know that walk is a sexy gait. Walk isn't a pushover because developing a saucy solid walk is hard work.

Depending on who you talk to, walk may be the most important gait. Competitors in Western, English Pleasure, Huntseat, and Dressage are judged at the walk. Years ago, many Western Pleasure horses were trained to walk by moving one foot, pausing, moving another foot, pausing, repeating the irritating pattern until asked to jog or lope. Someone decided that slow was always best, so s-l-o-w-e-r must be b-e-t-t-e-r.

Increased speed is often caused by imbalance, so yes, doing higher level maneuvers more slowly, with greater collection, can indicate a greater degree of difficulty. Most of the time, however, excessively slow speed kills the beauty and quality of any gait.

While judging a show in eastern Washington State, one particular horse entered the pen so slowly I turned away in disgust, noting on my card that the horse couldn't perform one of the three required gaits, the walk. As luck would have it, I placed the horse second in a class of eighteen head, telling the steward, "I don't want to do this, but I don't have any choice. I dinged this horse 30% because of the walk, but it was just that much better than the rest. I wish I could explain what I did over the loud speaker. Everyone will think that the stupid non-walk is good because the horse did so well."

Observers think they know why horses win or lose, but they're not always right. After a pleasure class at a World Show, one exhibitor turned his horse into the rail before lining up in the center of the pen. Everyone else turned toward the center which has long been the norm.

The exhibitor who turned his horse into the rail before lining up won the class. By the end of the two-week show, every rail rider turned his or her horse into the fence, thinking it would somehow improve their performance. I watched it happen, shaking my head in amazement. Clothing and tack styles change for similar reasons. At another World Show, men wearing solid jewel-tone shirts won the first few classes. The next season, every rider wore solid jewel-tone shirts with matching saddle blankets.

Because, of course, the color and pattern of what the rider wears must affect how well the horse performs. Not.

If your horse *isn't* quiet, obedient, fluid, and a joy to ride at the walk, why trot?

The Benefits of Walk

Increased speed means reduced response time. Walking gives you more time to think before you ask or correct, and choose the best response to the unexpected.

Walk is the perfect gait to introduce new concepts or maneuvers. It's valuable when experimenting with your horse's response to different cues, basic conditioning, building relationship and muscle memory. Every ride should begin with walking, warming up soft tissues and joints, and visiting with your horse to see if she's having a mediocre day, good day, or fabulous day. Is her head gently nodding from side to side in rhythm with her body? Is her tail moving freely from side to side?

Is she happy, comfortable, and ready to do something more?

I began to appreciate the beauty and challenge of Walk in my thirty-second year of horse training. Youth and strength let you get away with a lot, but eventually age motivates you to get smarter, give up, or risk getting broken.

Age and infirmity forced me to seek new information, skills, and options.[36]

I have a love/hate relationship with ground poles. They're amazing tools to improve horse and rider skills and they're fun. Endlessly riding around an arena gets boring for me and my horses, opening the door to sloppy habits and lack of precision. I love how ground poles break the monotony, making lessons more profitable and enjoyable.

What I hate about ground poles is carrying them into the arena to set up patterns, then putting them away when

-----

[36] Job 12:12, Proverbs 20:29,

I'm done. Wood poles are heavy, expensive, and require maintenance. Even when I leave them in the arena I still have to move them to drag the ground and replace them for the next ride.

Every year it takes more energy to groom and tack up. The thought of hauling around mini-utility poles throws cold water on more inspired riding options. I confess, some days are exercises in willpower, forcing myself to get up from my comfy, clean, climate-controlled office to make the fifteen second trek to the barn.

Sounds easy, right? What's fifteen seconds? Well, nothing if I'm already dressed in riding britches and boots, slathered in sun screen, and armed with hat, hood, or visor. Visiting the barn is easy. Saying "hi" requires nothing but temperature-relevant clothes and flip-flops or slip-ons.

Training is a completely different animal from just dropping by. I love riding, blissfully spending hours with the horses once I'm out the door and the first horse parked by the tack room door. Dragging logs requires a whole 'nuther level of mental preparation.

My preference is a series of four walk poles, spaced 28–32 inches apart. To make small adjustments easier when a horse moves one out of place, I measured the distance my horses prefer and marked a short whip with duct tape. I use walk-overs in hand, on the longe, and under saddle.

The possibilities are endless, and the benefits are amazing.

Asking a horse to down shift from canter to walk is easy once he sees the ground poles coming up. I time my cue and, Voila!—perfect transition. Okay, not every time, but I don't have to nag, tug on the longe line, or move out of place in liberty work. Visual objects make natural impressions on a horse, making ground poles one of your best friends.

———————

"Any time a horse needs to un-learn a poor postural habit — crookedness, stiffness, hollowness — he should spend plenty of time training at the walk. This gait, especially when used in conjunction with cavaletti, allows for training the nervous system to adopt new habits without interference from the larger gymnastic muscles that take over during gaits with more impulsion."

Jec Ballou

Walk Poles

10 Benefits of Using Walk Poles

1. Teaches automatic speed control, slowing chargey horses
2. Helps your horse anticipate transitions in a good way
3. Allows your horse to teach himself collection and stride length
4. Creates mental discipline and the habit of thinking
5. Keeps your horse's brain from going AWOL, spinning somewhere else
6. Connects your horse's feet to his legs to his body to his brain
7. Enhances responsiveness to your cues/aids/eyes
8. Teaches your horse to be accountable for where and how he travels
9. Improves physical balance, because all four legs have to work equally
10. Builds symmetry: mental, spatial, physical, energy

If you think about it, most behaviors and maneuvers you ask for make no sense to your horse. Tracking a cow makes sense. Jumping a vertical makes sense. Spinning in place or performing flying lead changes have no connection to the simple practical mind of a horse.

The benefits of walk poles exist because the horse teaches himself. Don't micro-manage or offer your horse a crutch. Some horses figure it out in one short session while others need a week of rapping toes, stepping on rails, or tripping. The greatest boon to every future lesson begins when your horse engages his brain, connects his feet to the ground, and figures out how everything works together.

I introduce walk poles on the ground, first leading the horse through a few times to let him know I expect him to remain cadenced and keep moving. The next step is working on a longe line or at liberty. Be sure you can guide your horse where you want and keep him moving before adding obstacles. Don't let him ditch, avoid, or refuse to engage the poles repeatedly.

Like any obstacle, once your horse engages the walk poles, DO NOT correct him or intrude. Let him figure it out. Like people, horses must learn how to learn. The easiest exercise is walk poles. Once your horse masters it, progress will be quicker and smoother when you introduce more complicated puzzles and exercises.

How to walk poles with your horse in-hand:

Keep your eyes up and walk toward a fixed point. Don't look down or back at your horse. Expect him to follow. Teach your horse to walk over the center of the poles from the beginning. That means you stay off to one side, so his feet pass over the center, not yours. If his leading skills are rusty, work on that first. Don't pull or correct. With every new maneuver or exercise, horses get participation awards for just showing up!

Your first goal is getting to the other side of the walk poles without getting involved.

How to ride walk poles:

Ride walk-poles the same way you engage a line of jumps. Identify your path to the center of the walk poles and once lined up, keep your eyes level, look straight ahead, and let your horse carry you where you're looking. Don't look down and don't worry if your horse hits a rail, moves crooked, or loses form.

Again, your goal is getting to the other side of the walk poles without getting involved. Short of an emergency, leave your horse alone. Stay out of his mouth, off his sides, and sit quietly. If your horse tries to move smoothly but frequently misses the last pole, try adjusting the spacing.

Let your horse teach himself. This is hard. If you have to, tie a bandana over your chin or do something else to remind you to be a passenger when your horse engages the poles. Guide your horse to the center line, get out of the way, then lightly engage again on the far side. The entire exercise should be stress-free and easy. Clunky is fine. Tense isn't.

Like any work, keep it fun and fresh. Horses get sloppy when they're bored, just like you. I mix up patterns before and after the poles, changing from circles to reverses to pivots. Walk or ride the poles in both directions. Can you get a smooth reverse by changing only your eyes and leg position? When walking, is your turn to the right as pretty and correct as your turn to the left? Walk poles teach your horse to think. Don't waste the opportunity.

Whether you lead or ride your horse, walk your poles ten to twenty times to warm up or as therapy. Invite a friend over to play. I learned bunches about using ground poles from Jec Ballou, who learned from Ingrid Klimke. We all learn from one another.

Best Energy—Saving Tip

NOT setting up poles is tempting when riding time is limited, you haven't had a caffeine fix since your morning coffee seven hours ago, or you just don't want to. When I have barely enough motivation to groom, saddle, and get in a basic maintenance lesson, lifting and toting ground poles doesn't make the cut.

One of the truths of life is that a saddled horse is a ridden horse. When I'm not hot to trot, tired, unmotivated, or tempted to skip a horse or two, I make a point to saddle every horse I hope to ride. Once saddled, the ride is a sure thing.

Now, you know that I love using walk-overs and other cavaletti patterns, but hate to pull, tote, rake, and measure. I overcame this conflict with a simple common-sense solution I discovered in a Jec Ballou article. Duh. I knew this but forgot I knew it.

Place your walk-over poles in a place you can leave them, out of the way of normal traffic patterns.

My poles are set up on the paddock side of the arena fence on level ground. They live there 24/7, always available, no muss and no fuss. My four walk-poles are centered outside the arena fence, with twenty-foot gates on either end, making it simple and convenient as a warm-up or to refocus a horse who's gotten ahead of the program. All I have to do is ride out one gate, over the walk poles, and back in the next gate.

I was completely surprised the first time I added walk poles to a full lesson. Q, our twenty-one-year-old gelding in rehab, learned the walk overs quickly, striding long and low, balancing equally on all four legs (the benefit I hoped for most) with greater confidence than he'd shown before. After warming up we trotted a circle, transitioning back to walk when we got back to the poles. I expected Q to handle the walk overs the same way after trotting as he did two minutes earlier.

He did not.

Q stumbled over two of the poles. Thinking it might be a fluke, we walked the poles a few times until Q walked them cleanly. We trotted again. Same result; he tripped. Which, once I thought about it, makes sense. Q performed the walk poles perfectly until I asked him to do something that shoved him right back into movement and habits I hope to fix. Repetition over days and weeks creates muscle memory and fitness. Habits and compensations accumulated over months and years don't disappear in a day.

Allow your horse adequate time to make permanent changes in balance, symmetry, and concentration habits. Listen to your horse. He'll tell you when it's time to add something new. Use your walk-poles every time you play with your horse, even if all you do is lead him across a few times before turnout.

Walk Poles and Barn Sour Horses

None of my horses are barn sour, but none are above cheating a little when they see an opening. They used to lean toward the barn on the north end of our outdoor arena. Expanding my working area to include my small indoor pen in the barn with the large outdoor helped eliminate that annoying habit. I have walk or trot poles set up inside, returning frequently to ride the poles a few times before heading right back outside.

My horses no longer pull toward the barn, leaking shoulders or hips, being resistant to rein or leg cues. The barn has ground poles, as does the paddock between the inside and outside arenas. Everywhere we ride there's an opportunity to do some easy, disciplined, thinking work; work that connects my horse's mind and body to mine.

"Within France's rich equestrian tradition, the walk has always deserved to be called the "queen of gaits" because of the benefits that both horse and rider can derive from this gait. The great François de Lubersac, a master from the legendary School of Versailles in the 18th century, recognized that in dressage training, the first gait in which to train is always the walk. Remarkably, de Lubersac, trained his horses only at the walk, and when he decided that they were ready, his horses were able to do everything at all gaits."

Dressage Today,
Colonel Christian Carde with Silke Rottermann

Warm Up Properly

Years ago, I discovered that Asti, our gorgeous black quarter horse mare, needed at least twenty minutes of warm up before I could get an accurate read on her body and brain for the day. Asti is laid back and quiet when you first get on, which I appreciate because I don't longe or round pen first. I figured she didn't need a lot of warm up; a perfect lady from her first step and seldom offered contrary opinions.

However, I learned that Miss Asti needed a l-o-n-g warm up before she was fully present in the moment. After twenty sweet minutes Asti's energy level shot from first gear to overdrive. Once warmed up, her stride lengthened, her leg speed quickened, her head came up and she wanted to "talk" about what the plan was for the rest of the ride. Once I figured this out, I changed Asti's lesson plans to take advantage of the slow times as well as the energetic ones. It didn't take long to harness her energy and the lesson is one I'll remember.

A proper warm up reinforces promises made and lessons learned. It's also less frustrating, safer, and far more relational.

After several years of declining ability, knee-replacement opened the gate to new experiences and discoveries in the world of horses. One of my early rehab habits that I continue today is walking on a treadmill with hand weights. A new world of horse training wisdom opened by walking on the treadmill because physical limitations forced me to set simple goals. As new ideas smacked me upside the head, I wrote them down in a notebook.

My thoughts and emotions regarding this new insight ranged from delight that I was regaining mobility and balance, to a hopeful shame when I realized how many times over the past quarter-century I misjudged a horse's inability as unwillingness. Everyone agrees that balance is a good thing. I knew about the importance of proper warm-ups, core training, and balance, but what I didn't realize is that I had great conceptual knowledge about all of them, but a less-than-stellar history of application.

I've gotten better.

Sometimes You Canter Before You Trot

Swizzle

Swizzle was one of my original amazing grays, a power-packed dappled gray mare with the most beautiful eyes I've ever seen. I learned a lot from Swizzle, some of which I'm still chewing on. It took a while to figure out that cute little Swizzle was far more comfortable cantering than trotting – especially in the warm-up phase. Like most of our horses, Swizzle was nearly as wide as she was tall; built more like a power lifter than a ballerina. Until fully warmed up Swizzle was stiff and sticky.

Most warm up programs begin slowly, gradually working up to faster gaits. Not Swizzle. She'd walk around like an Energizer Bunny with a failing battery, then bump into a canter. Swizzle couldn't always trot on a longe or at liberty in a round pen. She could walk and she could canter, but trot was always more difficult for her, proving that horses are as unique as we are.

When Swizzle's energy channels are open and flowing,

she trots well, nicely strided and forward. Sometimes cantering was a necessary step to get her energy flowing in a positive direction, producing a confident, pleasant trot with good cadence and balance. We made excellent progress once I realized Swizzle knew what she needed better than I did, reducing her warm up time by allowing her to do it the most efficient way for her. Instead of forcing her to warm up by the book, trot before canter, I let her decide what worked best. I listened to Swizzle as much as she tried to listen to me.

Bo

Bo is a wonderful teacher because sometimes he's smarter than I am. When I was just getting back into the saddle after four months off after surgery, I wanted to revisit relationship before moving on to lessons or performance goals. Bo was my first ride, so I let him warm up at whatever pace he chose. We walked around the arena getting our rhythm back.

Bo always begins a ride with his molasses-in-January walk, annoyingly slow, devoid of either impulsion or motivation. When I returned to riding with purpose with my upgraded knee, I wanted a little more effort. Bo's easy-going nothing-bothers-him manner was perfect for a disabled rider, but adding more energy to his walk would help to achieve greater consistency of cadence as the lesson progressed.

I figured Bo would need firm encouragement if I wanted him to invest more energy. After a couple of weeks in the arena we ventured into the pasture to walk and trot longer distances. I let Bo piddle along at the pace of a lame turtle. Interestingly enough, five or ten minutes later he moved into a more forward energetic gait all by himself. His ears livened up and he began working quietly and comfortably. I discovered that Bo didn't need to be pushed, because he volunteered once he warmed up.

Let your horse tell you what the best warm-up strategy is for him.

The Purpose of Warm Up

Asti used to require twenty minutes of warm up before I got a true reading on where she was physically and emotionally. Armed with that knowledge I listened to what she told me. After a few years her emotions no longer need a twenty-minute warm up, but as a more mature lady she needs time to get everything moving like it should. That's a reality we both share.

Swizzle never did anything by the book which is one reason she was such a blessing. God didn't create molds, popping out horses and humans that are carbon copies of all the others. Each is unique with something special to offer.

Bo is Bo. His steady personality and good will is a gift of faith that taught me to look in the mirror when we are out of step with each other rather than assume that he's the one who needs correction. The one who's out-of-kilter is usually me. Bo never says "No." If there was an emergency and we had to get somewhere fast right out of the chute, he would go. He can quicken his pace in the warm up, but only if I insist. I finally figured out that I have no business insisting. If there is no emergency, don't let your horse think there is.

I ask my body every day, "How ya doin'?" I learned that it pays to wait for the answer and proceed accordingly, or I might hurt something.

When your horse isn't the same today as yesterday, have you ever thought, "What's wrong with you? Who are you and what have you done with my horse? Yesterday you did this with no problem. Why won't you do it today?" Yesterday your horse responded perfectly to your light cue. Today he seems to have lost that file, your request nothing more than an irritating error code on an otherwise empty screen. He's not upset, resistant, or militant. He just isn't doing what you ask.

I've been there a hundred times, wondering what major upheaval happened to my wonderful horse since I put him up the day before. He isn't lame or sore. His disposition is as sunny as ever, eyes bright, engaged and willing—but there just isn't any going where I want to go.

My warm up experiences taught me to ask my horses, "How are you today" and wait for the answer before moving on. If your horse just can't go there, do something else.

It's possible to pull a horse out of the pasture cold and cowboy up. Some of those rides are great while others end with an emergency call to the veterinarian or rescue squad. The best results come after a proper warm up, both physical and relational. Build the habit of asking your horse how he feels and respect the answer. Amazing things happen when your mind, body, and spirit are ready to work with the mind, body, and spirit of your equine partner.

History Matters

People bring horses to me because something is transformed. I can do things with people's horses they can't. Now, before you think I have an over-developed ego, there's one distinct advantage I have over any owner having trouble with her horse; I'm not her.

History matters. When I meet a horse there's no baggage, expectation, disappointment, assumption, or resentment. The horse and I both begin with clean slates. I don't know or care what happened last week or last year. All that matters is what I see and feel. The horse knows nothing about me either, so tests, considers, and responds to what I'm doing, not what I did or didn't do earlier.

Tracy's grandparents bought her a twelve-year-old stocky bay Appaloosa gelding with beautiful markings. Like most kids, Tracy loved speed events, hoping to run barrels. She took lessons and made good progress with her horse — until she got scared. Everything was fine until it wasn't. Tracy got dumped when her horse did something unexpected. She got up and brushed herself off without as much as a bruise, but her confidence took a beating. She boldly jumped in the saddle to gallop any horse — except her own.

Her grandparents asked me to ride the horse for a few weeks to see if I could figure out the problem and help get Tracy and her horse back in sync. After a little tune up and change in hoof angles he was ready to go. Tracy started taking lessons on her horse.

Her horse wasn't push button, but he was thoughtful and reasonable. She needed to girl up and tell him what she wanted and make him do it. Tracy was totally capable but didn't give clear direction. She was afraid her horse wouldn't obey, so decided it was safer to let him call the shots. Which makes no sense at all, but who among us hasn't behaved oddly when we feel insecure in a relationship?

In the middle of her first lesson Tracy announced, "I'm at a seven!"

"What do you mean? What's a seven?"

"On a scale of one to ten, that's how nervous I am."

"Why are you thinking about how nervous you are?"

"My last teacher wanted me to tell her how nervous I was. I figured you would want to know."

Everyone has their own way of doing things, but I didn't want Tracy constantly assessing the state of her nerves. I wanted her to have fun, be excited, challenged, and eager to progress, not fixated on her emotions.

"What are you nervous about?"

There wasn't anything to be concerned about. Her horse was well behaved, but she couldn't get past her old fright. She simply didn't trust this horse anymore. She rode with wild abandon on anything else with four legs and a tail, but not her horse. I'd like to say that I fixed the problem, but I didn't. The horse was fine and Tracy was talented, but the combination was doomed.

In 1990 I bought a cute little gelding named Harley, a sweet little horse that needed conditioning, better hoof care, and a tune up. The seller told me Harley didn't like men which I found curious but didn't think much about it. By the time Harley made one forty-year-old woman's dream come true, I told her that he didn't like men because it was true. She took Harley home and they lived happily ever after.

Lacey was a gorgeous golden buckskin mare with wide blaze and four stockings. *Flashy* only begins to describe her. I'd judged her for several years, packing kids and ladies around in English, Western, and trail classes. She was a little machine with a permanent short stride in the right front that kept her from being a seriously high dollar pony. The injury was old and cold and she wasn't sore, but would always have a slightly uneven trot.

I'd met Lacey's owner at shows but didn't speak with her much until she bred Lacey to one of my stallions. When it was time for Lacey to go back to work her owner was in the market for a jumping prospect at the same time I was looking for a lesson horse. I had one, so we traded. I got my lesson horse and she got her jumping prospect.

Buckskin is my husband's favorite color and Lacey was beautiful. I'd seen her safely teach and pack students with only basic skills. My husband wasn't a horse guy, so I thought Lacey would be the perfect lesson horse for him. The first day he could, my husband led her out to the arena, mounting up for his first ride while I was still tacking up in the barn. Hollering ensued. I ran to the end of the barn and looked out. My husband was struggling up from the ground and Lacey was running free.

"Are you okay?"

"Yes, but I think I broke some ribs." He did.

Once I knew he was mostly alright I asked the big

question, "What did you do?"

"I didn't do anything. The moment I got my leg over her she ran off bucking."

I admit, it was hard to believe. In the years I'd known her, Lacey never had a hair out of place. There had to be more to the story.

A couple of months later I rode the shuttle to the airport parking lot to pick up my car after judging a horse show. A man in the facing seat said, "Hey, I think I know you. You have Lacey now, right?" He was the trainer's boyfriend and knew Lacey well.

"Yeah, she's an interesting case. She hates men. Every time I got on, she bucked me off."

History matters.

Fearful Riders

As a rule, fearful riders ride nervous horses. I don't believe you can bluff a horse, but even if it's possible, it doesn't happen often. A horse knows when his rider is afraid, giving him the opportunity to take advantage of a timid rider or become a basket case himself.

Gifted instructors guide riders through an educational and experiential process to either eliminate fear or discover ways to manage it productively. Texas trainer Donna Waldrup has the gift.

"I've always been enamored with horses, of course, but as a *special* child, I didn't speak until I was three. According to my mother my first word was dog. I've always felt secure and safe with animals." Donna has a long history as an animal trainer, befriending and training everything from toads to chickens. She says, "Horses and cows are the hardest!"

Donna believes the most important skills necessary to work with horses are patience, empathy, and knowing that less is more. "Horses have different personalities", she says, "but all come with the same natural instincts. Riding a horse for the first time is mostly about gathering information, building the *back story* about the horse, evaluating responses and looking for triggers." Donna tries to meet each horse where it is, then figure out what it needs from her. She listens when horses speak, working to open the lines of communication. She says, "I don't always agree with a horse, but I've learned how to debate without escalating or engaging anyone's emotions."

"I love helping fearful riders," whether they started that way or developed fear after an accident or scare. "We all have fears, but some folks allow it to control them. Fear equals lack of control. Besides, there's no such thing as a one hundred percent bomb-proof horse that's still breathing."

Sometimes people get hurt because they trust their horse. Or, as Donna suggests, they humanize their horse incorrectly. She knows that horses buck, bite, and paw as part of their system of communication.

I've known Donna for years and believe she can ride about any horse able to carry her. She's an armed forces veteran, comfortable with firearms, preaching the gospel, and is horse savvy. Donna is as fluent in the language of horse as I am. Yet she says, "I'm afraid every time I throw my leg over a horse, but I developed enough confidence to handle the situation and face my fears because I practice, practice, practice."

Donna helps nervous riders learn the skills to face their own fears by building up their tool boxes. Hesitant riders need to learn what to do first and then practice. She teaches them to listen to their horse, to sit properly, to use their hands, and use their legs the right way when trouble hits.

You can learn the same skill set. Once you know *what* to do when, confidence grows and fear subsides. If you're afraid, you're in very good company. Now, all you need is the right teacher and a plan. The unknown is exciting, scary, or a bit of both. If you need help assembling your tool box, look for someone to help you select the right tools and use them correctly. Your first tools should be the knowledge of how horses think, feel, and react.

I asked, "Is the fear still there?"

Donna says it is. But she has a tool box that works. Maybe she's like a demolition expert. Every job involves a bomb, but they learn the skills to evaluate, respond, and defuse the danger. Donna is horse-crazy, loving them enough to conquer her fear.

————

Donna and I met years ago over lunch when local horse women who met in my Facebook group scheduled a meet up. She and I got together later to compare horse and ministry notes and have been friends since. We don't see each other often because of our schedules, but there's always something new to learn.

I was astonished to learn that she is ever afraid. Donna competes in mounted shooting, knows how to protect herself, and exudes confidence. There is no *norm* that describes horse women. We're not avatars, but warriors of love and purpose.

————

"In other words," [the horse] continued, "you can't ride. That's a drawback. I'll have to teach you as we go along. If you can't ride, can you fall?"

"I suppose anyone can fall," said Shasta.

"I mean can you fall and get up again?"

C.S. Lewis, *A Horse and His Boy*

Lynn Baber

Hooked by Horses

Janet Craig

I was flying! Galloping along the sandy sun-drenched beach, salty spray dampening my skin as pounding hooves struck turquoise-blue waves. Nothing else in my seven-year-old life was this exhilarating.

We met a young equine entrepreneur on our 1972 family vacation in Acapulco. He offered tourists horseback rides on the beach. I shamelessly begged my parents for a ride and they reluctantly agreed. I'm sure they expected the ride to be sedate, safe, and under their supervision. To their surprise, and I expect sheer terror, we raced down the beach and out of sight. The young man spoke little English and my parents even less Spanish, so the approved parameters of the ride weren't adequately communicated. In those days there were no cell phones, leaving my English-only parents standing alone on the beach, their elementary-school daughter stolen away by a man on a horse.

One can imagine their relief when we loped back into view. Rocking in the lap of magic from the first moment on horseback, nothing was further from my mind than concern for potential danger and frantic parents. I couldn't stop jabbering about my adventure—one I'm sure they preferred to forget.

But that was it. I was hooked.

My love for animals began much earlier, but one gallop

213

on the beach stirred what became a lifelong love of all things equine. Like a magnet, I was drawn to horses, jumping at the smallest opportunity to talk to them, touch them, or on very special occasions, even ride them. My family lived in the suburbs, so keeping a horse at home posed several problems. Time and again, I prepared and presented proposals to my father resolving the issues of paddock and stall space. Why not use the backyard and half of his garage? It made perfect sense to me, but somehow, he never saw it the same way I did.

With a limited budget and no stables near our home, I relied on friends with horses to scratch my equine itch. I never turned down the opportunity to visit someone who owned a horse that might let me ride. I thought that people who had horses were the luckiest people in the whole world.

I dreamt of riding, devouring every book on horses I could lay my hands on. My room was decorated in Early Equine, its centerpiece my collection of Breyer models. When considering my career choices, I first thought being a jockey fit the bill but later decided that being a veterinarian would be even better. As a child, my soul was happy in the company of horses and it still is today. My favorite smells are horses, barns, and leather. But as years passed, my desire to have a horse of my own began to feel like a pipe dream, fanciful and unattainable.

In 1990 I married Philip, the love of my life, whose name means *lover of horses*. Twin boys arrived in 1994 and we were further blessed in 2002 with a daughter. As a suburban wife and busy mother of three, my dream of ever having a horse receded further. A lady up the road offered pasture rides for a price and I admit to sneaking off twice, leaving my husband with the kids while I indulged my passion for horses. It was a generous gesture on his part because our grocery budget couldn't stretch enough to include pasture rides. I did, however, pack up my children, carrots, and apple slices to visit the horses hoping to instill a love of horses in them. Isn't that what mothers do?

In May 2006, my precious daddy went home to be with the Lord. The loss was indescribable.

Twelve months later, I was diagnosed with Stage Two breast cancer. I remember thinking, *this is the end of my life – and my little daughter is only five years old.* I was angry with God, repeatedly telling Him how I felt about leaving my young family. As silly as this may sound, I realized that not only would I never have a horse of my own, I might not even have a life. I told God, as if I had any say in the matter, that He would have to take me kicking and screaming because I still had more living to do.

In case I didn't make it, I wrote and sealed four letters to my husband and each child before the first of seven surgeries and multiple rounds of chemotherapy. I'm pleased to report that I survived and remain in remission with no evidence of disease. Praise be unto God! After that I surrendered my horse dream, resigning myself to the obvious reality that horses weren't part of God's plan for my life. It was a tough pill to swallow, but I was grateful to be alive and still with my family. But that's not where the story ends.

In 2013 my husband became the Executive Director of a Christian conference center, retreat, and summer camp. The facility had an existing herd of nine horses in varying degrees of utility and no manager. Somehow, I got the job of Equestrian Director, was certified as a riding instructor, and my real education began. Several years later I knew a lot more about horses and believed the accommodations for our herd needed improvement.

I started a GOFUNDME account to enable the camp to build a real barn for the horses. Everything was outside; watering, feeding, and cleaning, the only covered areas were where I tacked and hitched horses for riders and the small protective roofs in the paddocks. In ice storms the horses got covered and so did I. When Texas winds blew sideways, so did we. While waiting for sufficient funding from that campaign and other fund-raising projects we cleaned paddocks and replaced fencing.

Today we have a fourteen-stall raised center aisle barn with indoor feed room, tack room, and water sources. I not only have one horse, but fourteen! It's some of the hardest work I've ever done, but also some of the most rewarding. God faithfully placed people and resources along my journey to help accomplish His purpose. I'm alive, grateful, and blessed by the connections He continues to supply.

Six years later I'm still camp Equestrian Director, the best job ever. I've learned the importance of patience and pacing because this is a marathon, not a sprint. Every dream comes with challenges; a herd of horses requires commitment, common sense, consistency, being honest with yourself and everyone else, a willingness to learn, and lots of prayer. And love.

Years ago, I gave up on my dream, but it wasn't really over. Even on the hottest summer days wrangling horses and kids, when my energy levels are sorely taxed, the love of horses and the opportunity to serve get me up each day to tromp out and feed, count noses, and prepare for another day.

And I still have my entire Breyer model horse collection. God is GOOD!

Janet and I met not long after she accepted the responsibility for the horses at camp. Her passion and dedication are only matched by her selfless devotion and love of all of God's creation, especially horses, children, and Philip. The example she and Philip set is a joy to witness and personally inspiring.

Like many women who realize their horse dreams later in life, Janet hit the ground running and never looked back, moving from dedicated newbie to knowledgeable and equine-savvy, being soft when soft is needed and firm when it's the better way, all topped with a big side order of creativity. Janet is tiny, tough, resilient, and expressive. Her love of all animals and children is as exceptional as her love for the Lord. I am blessed to call her my friend.

"Whatever you do, work at it with all your heart, as working for the Lord, not for men."

Colossians 3:23

Lynn Baber

The Pony Finger

Horses are wonderful, obedient, sweet, obstinate, frustrating, challenging, joyous, fulfilling, and obsessive. Most are creative communicators capable of telling you precisely where to scratch, what perfume is most annoying, which treat is the bomb, and when you've ticked him off or hurt his feelings.

Occasionally, he expresses his annoyance by giving you The Pony Finger. Horses only have one toe, unable to flip symbolic gestures, but perfectly capable of communicating disgust, disdain, or displeasure.

Bo and I hadn't hauled out for months. In past years we competed in Mounted Shooting, turned back cattle, rode trails, went to church and ministry events. Bo also serves as my assistant and easy chair when I teach clinics.

I thought Bo should come along when I started working with the equestrian director at a local Christian camp. If I needed a working horse, he'd be right there and maybe we'd get to check out the wooded trails. I set up a pen for him at camp a week earlier so he'd have a safe, comfy place to chill. The first week he jumped in the trailer and we headed south.

We only worked with camp horses that day, so I didn't need Bo, only managing to sneak in a five-minute bareback ride before leaving. Bo got back into the trailer and everything appeared copacetic.

The next week, Bo was a little stickier getting into the

trailer, but not a problem. Again, I didn't do much with him during the day, so he grazed in his pen until it was time to head home. How could that be a bad thing for a horse?

The third week Bo balked at the open door, settling his great white body outside the trailer, telling me that going in was not his first choice. The camp director expected me at a particular time and I didn't want to be late. Bo, it seems, had his own schedule. I asked. He loaded. Then immediately backed out. He wasn't interested in going to camp because he didn't get to participate.

"Look, all you do is haul me down there and ignore me. If that's all you're doing, I'm not going."

Bo's message was clear. He's 99.99% fearless, obedient, and dependable, but gets ruffled tail feathers when he feels slighted. Bo isn't a drama king at all, reserving snit fits for this one situation. He and I have been here before. Standing outside the trailer with my indignant Great White Horse, I remembered the last time Bo didn't want to load.

A few years earlier my husband and I traveled to Oklahoma for a ministry event. I was scheduled to present a round pen demonstration during both the morning and afternoon sessions. I used Bo in the morning to demonstrate the benefits and concepts of a solid relationship, from ground pen liberty exercises to riding bareback with imperceptible cues. Toward the end of the program an audience member asked a few questions then said,

"I wish you could work with my mare."

"Where is she?"

"Three miles down the road."

"If you can get her here, we'll work with her this afternoon."

Working with a horse I've never met lets the audience know how introductions are made and was a great contrast to the morning demonstration. Bo is my horse, so everyone expected him to be attentive. The mare and I were strangers but she reacted the same way Bo did. The mare's owner and his son realized that the trouble they had with their beautiful palomino mare wasn't her problem, it was their problem.

Seeing the process of change is far more powerful and instructive for audiences. It was a good day and we were jazzed. To quote one of our veterinarians, "I love it when a plan comes together."

Bo spent his afternoon chilling in a pen with water and snacks. When I asked him to load up for the journey home, he refused. This was the first time Bo ever refused *anything*. I bought Bo as a two-year-old who was never haltered. Years later, I was still the only person who'd ever tacked and ridden him. But this particular afternoon he was miffed. I'm fluent in horse, with not the slightest doubt what Bo was telling me;

"You want someone to load up in your trailer? Why don't you ask the horse you spent your entire afternoon with? If I wasn't good enough then, don't think I'm going to play good pony now just because you ask."

I was stunned. This was so unlike my reliable, agreeable, dependable Bo. Horses it seems, like people, have little snippets of personality that pop out when least expected. Every horse professional knows what it's like to have a horse give them the Pony Finger. Here I was, the clinician, having to discuss getting in the trailer with my own horse. I hoped no one was watching.

Humility and horses are a package deal.

Just as he did in Oklahoma, Bo didn't feel valued by hauling to camp and being ignored. He saw no point in loading to go do nothing. I understood his feelings, but he doesn't get to decide when he gets into a trailer and when he doesn't.

Bo got in, then immediately put his massive frame into reverse and was out. I asked him to get back in. He got in, then slammed his tranny into reverse again. He toyed with me, his displeasure obvious. When asked, I expect Bo to get in and stay in. He communicated perfectly; he was not going to play.

The Pony Finger is not an acceptable form of communication from your horse any more than the human equivalent is from your teenager. We weren't going there again. Bo didn't want to get into the trailer to go to camp and I had to leave to get there on time.

Did I give up, give in, or put Bo away?

Not exactly.

Bo didn't go to camp with me. I walked him back to his stall and tied him to the rail. I petted him and said I'd see him when I got back. My husband was home, so I told him that Bo was tied in his stall and to leave him there until I got back. He was inside under a fan, standing on comfy rubber mats with shavings. He could take a nap, rethink his behavior, or just hang out. If anything happened, my husband would be sure he was okay.

I drove to camp in my Jeep. After a wonderful three-hour visit I returned home. Bo was napping in his stall. After a short break I untied him, offered him a drink, and headed back to the trailer. Bo gets into horse trailers with or without a ramp. Stock or slant. Big or small. All he lacks is the motivation to change his "No, I won't!" into "Sure, whatever you say." That's where I come in.

I asked Bo to load up the way I always do. He didn't. I asked again. He didn't. We walked back to his stall and I tied him up again.

"See you in a while. Take another nap."

I don't fight with horses or smack 'em around. Years spent training stallions taught me other ways to make a point. I'm in the wrong weight class to wrestle a horse, but I know a bunch of ways to get into their heads. Bo didn't need help, he needed a reason to load. I was offering him a reason. Load or chill in his stall; his choice.

The third time was the charm. I untied Bo, offered him a drink, and walked out to the trailer like it was the first time.

"Load up."

He did.

I latched him into the slanted stall and drove him around the block. Where I live, it's a big block. When we got home, Bo politely backed out of the trailer and I turned him loose with his herdmates. The Pony Finger went into mothballs.

No muss, no fuss, no drama.

It was a good day.

Horses Read Your Mind

Horses can read minds, but most don't want to. For good reason. Most of us have messy minds. Cluttered collections of emotions, to-do-lists, wonderments, and self-talk, all in constant motion. We juggle thoughts, worries, and bits of conversation that won't leave us alone.

I meet with the Lord every morning. Beginning with prayer, I tell Him what's on my mind and listen for anything He has for me. Then it's on to Bible study and other related reading. At least that's the plan. Too often I discover I'm thinking about something completely unrelated to what I sat down to do. Somehow, in mid-conversation with God Himself, my mind wanders away. Again.

The same thing happens when I'm riding, my intention is to be fully present, aware of my breathing, focused on where we're going next, tuned-in to my horse's body and energy, centering my weight, attempting to say more without a conscious cue than with.

I need to trim around the pasture obstacles. There are weeds on Tire Mountain. It looks messy. I wonder if I put on enough sun block? Where did Laura say we were having lunch tomorrow?

My horse's lack of precision draws me back to what I'm doing—riding. At least it looks like I'm riding and doing a fair job but my horse isn't fooled. He knew the precise moment my thoughts left *us* and wandered *out there*. When I quit paying attention, so did he.

Why is staying on task so hard? It takes self-discipline and practice to manage the content and direction of our thoughts. Who teaches this? Schools? Churches? Self-help books? Horses learn because they're motivated. Change requires incentive. There must be a reason to go from here to there. I don't get out of bed in the morning because I'm bored, but because something else means more than ten blissful minutes of extra sleep.

Wouldn't it be lovely if your horse read your mind and did what you thought? It's possible, but rarer than a guilt-free gooey chocolate cake. Do you remember a brilliant moment where you and your horse were one hundred percent on the same wavelength? His breath was your breath. His spirit your spirit. It doesn't happen often, does it? But it can happen more consistently.

Star Trek fans (we're of that certain age) remember the Vulcan Mind Meld. Spock spread his fingers between someone's ear and forehead, linking his mind to theirs. Speech isn't necessary. Secrets are revealed. Emotions in one are felt by the other. According to Star Trek lore, only Vulcans can mind meld, ordinary folks can't. I disagree. Have you mind-melded with a horse? It's ridiculously rare. Mind melding is largely myth. Most folks can't do it because only a precious few are motivated enough to learn how, with the self-discipline to practice.

One day my husband rode Ace in our indoor pen. It isn't a huge area, but perfect for ground work and adequate for most simple riding lessons. I was working to build an entirely new mindset in Ace from the one he came with. He arrived with dissociative disorder, where pressure sent his mind to a faraway universe where communication was impossible.

Ace made great progress and Baber (my husband) loves him. The goal was walking a simple pattern, alternating riding the rail and changing directions on the diagonal. Same pattern. After a few minutes Ace seemed less secure. He was tight, jerky, and wandering around instead of staying on course. My husband was concentrating hard, riding the pattern in his mind. Making sure he did it right. Ace gathered speed, raising his head as his anxiety grew, searching for help. My husband was still concentrating, but not riding the pattern.

"Baber, go ahead and stop."

"What? Why?"

"Don't you feel Ace getting nervous?"

"No."

"He is. What are you trying to do?"

"I'm riding the pattern, just like you told me to."

"But Ace isn't doing the pattern anymore."

The surprised look on his face told me that he was oblivious to what was happening underneath his seat.

"What? I'm concentrating as hard as I can. What's wrong with him?"

"Nothing. You're so busy doing the pattern in your head you forgot to include Ace."

Baber fixated on the wrong input, thinking more about where he wanted to go than who he was going there with. Ace tried to tell him he was getting lost, but my husband's mind was already fully involved elsewhere. It happens, especially to people who are detail oriented and highly committed.

Horses can also fixate on things without considering the rider. The second year we rode together, Journey's body tensed during a lesson in the outdoor arena. He stopped, looking over the fence to the far side of the neighbor's arena, laser-focused on something. It was a small black animal. Maybe a cat? Nothing that I thought should be of concern, but Journey disagreed. He was transfixed, trying to figure out what it was and if it was a threat. Horses don't like surprises, especially those with Journey's history.

Journey was spellbound by the animal, forgetting I was there. Anything I did would be a surprise, like me when shocked out of an engrossing novel. I jump when startled and I didn't want Journey to jump. Horse learn to multi-task the same as we do. They learn to listen to you, recognize the dog running in the yard, note the airplane high overhead, and keep it all together. Productive multi-tasking requires security.

Do you multi-task? It only works if you're not upset, scared, or fixated on one specific thing. You may be running a dozen things in your head until you slip on a wet floor, when one hundred percent of your brain kicks into the attempt to keep from falling.

In that way you're not so different from your horse.

Horses can read minds, but they seldom do. Most adult minds are ill-kept, messy, jumbles of emotion and random unrelated stuff. Our thoughts bounce around like fleas in a jar. Horses like peace. Simplicity. Clarity.

Be that.

Horses and Children

One reason kids and horses go so well together is

because they think alike; one thing at a time.

"Come here, Sunny."

Six-year-old Katie wants her pony Sunny to come closer. There's nothing in her tender mind except a picture of Sunny standing next to her. Sunny looks into Katie's mind, sees the simple picture and moves to her side.

Sixty-year-old Ellen wants her horse Captain closer. Captain takes a quick peek into Ellen's mind:

"Why aren't you over here where you should be? Are you dis-respecting me? I don't have time for this today. Did I forget to turn off the coffeepot? Yikes. I don't want to burn the house down. What am I going to get for dinner tonight? It's gonna be tight getting home in time to cook if I have to stop at the store."

"My left foot feels squashed. Maybe I need new boots. Shirley never answered my text. Is she mad at me? This sun is frying me. I forgot sunscreen. I have to go the bathroom."

Captain drops his head to nibble the grass. Ellen adds another thought, and it isn't pleasant. Captain visited her mind then made a quick exit. It's easier to wait for Ellen to make a big demand than figure out what she wants. *If she really wants me, she'll come over and put on my halter.*

Your horse doesn't ignore you because he's playing a game. At least not usually. He ignores you because your mind is a mess. Horse brains don't work like yours and eventually they quit trying. Horses don't read your mind because it's not a happy place.

Becoming as a little child isn't just a requirement for entering heaven.[37] It's imperative to relationship with horses.

Childlike Perspective

You and your granddaughter stop for gas and see a horse across the street. Your granddaughter squeals, "Horsee!"

You think, "Kinda long backed, chewed tail, probably needs to be wormed, but cool hind stockings."

Your granddaughter is in love. "Horsee" sums it up. Delight. Joy. Expectancy. She wants in.

You catalog what you see. You judge, assume, and think three negatives to every positive. You just want to get back on the road. Successful relationship with a horse requires simplicity. You must be able to think about one thing at a time. Emotions must be stilled and quieted.

Make your mind an inviting place to visit. Focus is key. Focus requires self-control.

---

[37] Matthew 18:3

Focus

Never underestimate the importance of proper focus. If you stare at the hood of your car while driving, you'll crash. Staring at your horse while riding isn't good either. You may not crash, but you and your horse can't dance together.

Focus means getting your attention off of YOU. When riding, focus on where you want your horse to take you, not on the horse. It's SO tempting to try to ride a horse's ears, the default for most new riders and experienced trainers who need a reminder. The older I get the more tempted I am to ride "close." The same thing happens when I drive. I'm as smooth as I used to be, but instead of the car going where it should, I have to make frequent small corrections to stay between the lines. If my eyes stray to the right to look at a pasture of new foals my car is prone to head that way as well. There are many creative things about aging. This is one of them.

Recently I realized I was driving close. Instead of easy graceful curves and precise straightaways I drove a series of fast sharp corrections. When I realized what I was doing, I looked way ahead to the center of the lane like I used to. I remembered what it was like riding twisty mountain roads on my motorcycle, planning my line, riding forward, miles passing effortlessly, becoming one with the bike. I didn't steer the bike as much as it responded to my thoughts.

Which sounds a lot like riding a horse. One Monday my husband groomed the arena with the Kawasaki Mule dragging the harrow. Instead of monotonous exercises, Ace and I tracked it like a steer.

What fun! I enjoyed beautiful consistent gaits from a horse who returned home after a nine-year absence with dissociative disorder. For the first time, Ace softly responded to tiny cues. I FOCUSED on the Mule instead of micromanaging Ace. We rode straight lines and sweeping curves, moving with purpose, forward and engaged because of the Mule and not my irritatingly insistent leg cues. I relaxed and let Ace move out at the pace he found comfortable to stay safely positioned ten to twenty feet behind the harrow.

Ace's leg speed was constant as a metronome, his body balanced, and his spirit willing. He was open and entertained, happy, and focused on the same thing I was. It was a new high with a horse. The Mule helped me realize that my focus needed a reboot, which changed my riding plans for the next couple of horses.

I quit riding "close." I rode for the horizon, seat open, smiling and breathing consciously and freely. The more I focus on where I want to go the more naturally my horses take me there. Focus becomes fun when you and your horse work together. I wasn't telling them what to do as much as sharing a dance.

Focus is key, but it's hard. Focus requires discipline, the product of motivation and habit. Even then, it's not a sure thing. Sometimes I forget, falling into a rut or bad habit without intention because I fail to properly focus.[38] It's equally important in relationship with God. If you're consumed with excessive detail or over-think, you miss the

---

[38] 1 Peter 1:14, Psalm 119:30, James 1:2, Acts 2:28, Proverbs 4:25

joy. Perfect moments with a horse happen when minds, spirits, and bodies come together. Unity brings obedience without thought.

Recently I watched a liberty video of the legendary entertainer and horse trainer, Tommy Turvey, performing at a major event. The act consisted of Tommy, two paint horses, and a lady I assume is Mrs. Turvey. One horse was supposed to work with him and the other with Mrs. Turvey.

Mrs. Turvey and her horse did well, but Tommy's horse blew him off, and not just a little. For the entire show, Tommy's horse didn't even pretend to pay attention. Tommy tried to put a good face on it, but his horse flat out ignored him. Tommy attempted to draw him back time and again but it didn't work. The horse's behavior was blatant, a Pony Finger for all to see.

I loved that video because it's real. I don't know about you, but every now and again I experience focus failure. So do my horses. Is the horse wrong or did I mess up? Maybe neither. Magic is just that because it happens when two hearts, spirits, bodies, and egos move in unity. It's not the stuff of every day.

Focus Failure

Everyone experiences focus failure. It's important to build a "focus" cue into your horse's foundation. The habit builds over time until it's more a reaction than response. It's ready when you need your horse to snap back to you without thinking. It could save your life.

Teaching doesn't happen in the midst of crisis. Experience happens. It doesn't matter what perceived trouble appears if your horse's focus is squarely on you because he knows he's safe with you. Keeping him with you — remaining focused — is critical.

Focus failure is a fact of life. Nothing kicks off day-dreaming like prayer, remembering ten minute later that you were supposed to be praying, not working on next week's project list. We screw up, realize what we've done, then wonder, "What will God think of me?"

I feel for Tommy, but horses are like that. Horses don't concentrate perfectly all the time and neither do you. If your horse's mind wanders or he gives you the Pony Finger, don't feel like you're less than you are. Even the best, like Tommy Turvey, have days like that.

Tommy still loves his horses.

God still loves you.

Your horse still loves you, too.

Obedience

"The revelation of my growth in grace is the way in which I look upon obedience. We have to rescue the word 'obedience from the mire."

Oswald Chambers

Obedience is a gift.

If you've been in the horse community more than fifteen minutes you know folks disagree on major points. Some believe leadership is always abusive and that every request for obedience from a horse is punitive.

I endorse Master-Follower relationships, but only when the master is worthy and the follower volunteers. Horses are hard-wired from birth to seek herdship, build upon established hierarchical roles, and to follow a leader. Foals follow their mothers because they're born with the instinct to follow. Security and life are found with mother. The mothers follow the herd leader because they know the importance of herdship.

I never want a horse to GIVE UP his will, but to EXERCISE his will and choose me.[39]

Obedience always includes the opportunity to not obey. Leading a horse who chooses to follow doesn't require a halter or rope and you don't have to turn around

---

[39] 2 Corinthians 9:7, Philippians 3:12, John 8:36

to see if he's still behind you. When Jesus says, "Come", eyes meet, and our feet move in His direction. When Jesus says, "Follow Me" He turns and strides toward His destination. He never sneaks a peek to see who's coming.

If you ask your horse to come and feet don't move, work on the relationship. Motivate his will, not his won't. If you ask him to follow and he doesn't, give him a reason to WANT to follow.[40] Every horse in my barn is here by my choice. Every shred of obedience gifted to me is their choice, but I have to earn it. Obedience is *will on the hoof*, activated and alive. Some days your horse softly says "yes" to your every request. Those are priceless.

On other days your horse hesitates. Does he still choose to obey when he doesn't understand? When what you ask is hard? What about you? Are you ever whiny, stubborn, rebellious, reluctant, or confused? Relationship with a horse isn't once and done. I earn my position daily. I'm a fanatic about never breaking a promise to one of my horses. I'm not perfect, but I do my best to let them think I am. Perfectly fair, just, loving, consistent, and concerned for them.

Obedience must include the option to not obey. Anything else is coercion; it sure isn't love.

Horses cherished by a worthy master are blessed. Cared for by One who never disappoints. Jesus doesn't ask us to give up our will, but to exercise it—in relationship with Him.

---

[40] Psalm 40:8

Criticism and Correction

Let's be honest, who eagerly seeks criticism? My first reaction to someone who tells me I failed to live up to her standard isn't a warm fuzzy unless I asked for her opinion. "You should NEVER wear that color!" *Okay, thank you, but I like this color.* Criticism can be beneficial, but only when used with wisdom and love.

Too many people believe that correction and criticism are synonymous when they really have nothing in common. Effective compassionate leaders consider the needs of others before their own, designing lessons and activities to maximize the follower, whether human or horse. At best, criticism is an observation tied to a well-intentioned suggestion. At worst, it's a judgment without benefit.

The flip side of "reward every try" is penalizing genuine effort, which strangles motivation. Horses learn to quit when honest efforts are punished.

How long would you stick around if someone asked you for something, you try your best to give it, but all you get for your effort is:

"No!" (Slap.)

"No!" (Slap.)

"No!" (Slap.)

Criticism informs you that you aren't doing something the way someone else wants you to. Punishment adds something punitive to the equation while correction shares the opportunity for improvement and guides you in the right direction.

After a rich active life together, Q was retired to pasture when Susan's health worsened. After eighteen years away, several years without work, and an ego the size of Texas, he arrived with no muscle tone and a handful of soundness issues. Q is smart and creative, and more than willing to teach people his preferences.

Once we made the decision to ship Q home, I asked his owner if he had any bad habits. "Be honest. He's coming home no matter what you tell me."

She mentioned a few.

Then another two or three.

Then a few more.

The veterinarian who did a pre-transport health check called to let me know that Q didn't like vaccinations. So much so, that he "reared up and looked right at me." She's a good hand with horses and held her own, but she believes Q deliberately threatened her.

No problem. I wanted to know the worst Q had up his spotted pony sleeve so he wouldn't get any foreseeable opportunity to misbehave. When the now old man arrived, I hoped he might remember me fondly and renew our relationship on that level.

Smart horses test people and Q is an insanely smart horse. From the day he arrived home it was game on. He tried to step on my feet when I groomed him, pretending it was an accident, "Oh so sorry, I was looking at the dog next door." Q tried to push past me in the stall, hoping I'd think he couldn't focus because this was all so stressful and new to him and wouldn't push back. "What? Did you get crunched by the wall when I steamrolled past?"

I didn't get smushed but came close. And then that game stopped. He did fool me a couple times, head and neck up, ears pricked forward, holding his breath, completely engrossed in something off in the distance he saw out the breezeway door. The minute I dropped my guard he flipped around and took off the opposite way. He was just waiting for the right moment.

Q did that twice before I shut him down.

Q wasn't punished in his first three years and I won't start now. I offer motivation and the opportunity to choose behaviors. He's a smart guy and decided to get along. That's wonderful, but lovelier still is how Q offers affection, companionship, and now politely asks for attention.

Horses get a lot of criticism and way too much undeserved punishment. Why do we love horses so much? Because horses so seldom retaliate; choosing patience, perseverance, and grace when they could do serious damage, offering us the benefit of their doubt.

When a horse (or anyone) learns that their best effort gets the same result as no effort at all, it quits. There's no reason left to try. Every shred of motivation and good will is history. The relationship is bankrupt.

Since we're supposed to be the intelligent side of the horse–human equation, the buck stops on your shoulders. When your horse isn't behaving as you want, diagnose the cause and select the proper response:

- Motivation inspires and creates willingness.

- Correction intends to produce improvement.

- Punishment is used to extinguish dangerous behaviors.

If your horse's want-to isn't strong enough, choose and offer a higher-value motivator. Refer to the chapter, *What's In It For The Horse*. The way your horse should translate your correction is, "Let me help you with that."

Long before you're confronted with the need to punish, identify what behaviors deserve punishment and what you're prepared to do about it. What forms of punishment are you skilled enough to deliver effectively? Even when you try to scare a behavior clean out of a horse, you're still accountable for his safety and that of anyone else in the vicinity.

Reserve punishment for dangerous behaviors that jeopardize the safety of your horse, other horses, and people. Only use it when you're willing to put your horse in fear of his life, intending to kill the behavior once the horse realizes that he'd rather quit doing what he did to live another five minutes. Even then, be quick and then forgive him completely. Punishing lesser behaviors may coerce (dominate) your horse into doing what you want, but he won't love you for it.

The resulting emotion is resentment, anger, or fear; polar opposites of what we dreamed about as little girls drawing horses, reading Black Beauty's account of life as a horse, vowing to never let our own horse down—if we're lucky enough to get one. Women seek connection, affection, and shared understanding from their horses. Safeguard your precious relationship by helping your horse, not criticizing or punishing him.

Make love, not war.

Correction intends to mold and guide.[41] It's a loving positive response to an attempt that missed the mark from inability, not rebellion. Correction helps your horse move closer to your goal. Whenever I use the term, it is supportive, not synonymous with chastisement or punishment.

- Correction makes right things better.

- Correction promotes consistency.

- Correction sets boundaries.

A program of incremental corrections instructs, improves, and builds confidence. With horses and children, any movement in the right direction is a win. Celebrate with carrots, cupcakes, chocolate, and champagne!

Beginnings must be established before adding anything more complicated or precise. The two bookends supporting success with horses are commitment and consistency. Precision and correction are essential tools for building consistent experiences producing success, one little bitty step at a time. Every big success is the sum of a series of tiny successes. Consistency in the progressive mastery of skills is measured and planned.

Correction builds Confidence

Never correct an effort in progress. Let your horse commit to a mistake before you correct his performance. Correction isn't used to introduce or teach; it is used to

---

[41] 2 Timothy 3:16, Galatians 6:1, Proverbs 3:12

refine. Decide in advance where you'll step in with a correction. If you're teaching back-up (rein-back), which is most important, correct movement or straightness? Horses need to know what you're correcting. Don't try to fix two things at once. Have a plan and work it.

The proper use of correction builds confidence in one's ability to both understand a goal and to perform successfully. Using correction as a crutch builds confidence in the crutch, preventing healing and the return of strength, damaging self-confidence. The continuous use of a crutch weakens instead of builds.

If you always ride your horse with a restricting rein, you will always have to ride your horse with a restricting rein. Unless you give your horse the opportunity to fail, he will never learn to succeed without the crutch of your hand. The only way your horse will ever learn to ride with a loose rein, or no rein, is to ride with loose reins or no reins. The hands of a worthy master support and encourage; they do not serve as barriers to growth and confidence. The touch of grace empowers, it does not weaken.

Most women seek lifetime relationships. Blanket your horse with affirmation, designing lessons that showcase his or her strong points. Use correction as an opportunity to fix what isn't yet perfect, one tiny step at a time. Reward every try and be gob-smacked delighted with the smallest effort.

Every minute you spend with your horse is an opportunity to build commitment and grow trust. Learn to offer the gift of correction with wisdom and love. Commitment is the heartbeat of your dream.

THE BREATH OF HORSE CRAZY

Consistency

Children and horses are often taught that the rules of behavior at home differ from those expected in public. When new friends come over for Sunday dinner, you expect children to exhibit a higher standard of etiquette, restraint, and attention than they did the other 160-plus hours of the week.

Most parents know what it's like to flush with embarrassment when little Johnny or sweet Susie lets out with an unexpected dose of reality at the dining room table. Mind you, Johnny and Susie seldom sit at the dining room table because the good china only comes out of the pantry on special occasions.

Most competitors in equine events, whether breed, discipline, or community trail rides, have flushed with embarrassment when darling Prince or elegant Electra bucked, bolted, or ignored their request. Mind you, Prince and Electra seldom venture into competitive or social environments where they're expected to exhibit "company manners."

Distinguishing between family and company manners introduces compartmentalization, teaching that what's acceptable changes with circumstance. Johnny and Susie's parents model inconsistency, giving tacit approval to behavior that is less polite at home with the family. The kids learn that rules of behavior and etiquette aren't really rules. Put them with new people or in unfamiliar places and what they do becomes a crap shoot.

Horses can learn that different rules apply in different situations. Because I was consistent, one of my horses, General Silver, knew that a bridle with a bit meant he was a show horse while a bitless hackamore meant he was a working stiff.

At the time, General was smarter than me. He was one of my most influential teachers and I had to earn his respect and cooperation. General also knew how to push the envelope. Early one show season I signed up for a half-dozen classes at a big show. Things went well until clouds rolled in and dumped rain on us, a rare event in Arizona. We'd never ridden in the rain before, much less in competition, and darling General offered a brand-new behavior.

At the end of a rail class, the steward asked us to line up in the center of the arena facing the judges. We did. Sort of. General decided he didn't approve of the wet stuff and left no doubt about his feelings. Right there in the center of the show pen he stood up on his hind feet and waved at the crowd. My new black hat hit the mud. One of General's hooves squashed it flat.

General's otherwise good manners melted in the rain. There wasn't any point in going on, so we loaded up and went home. General stood tied while my husband put the other horses away and I pulled on my yellow Dry Rider suit, a remnant from my days riding motorcycles.

General and I went for a ride in the rain. He objected. The ride continued. General continued to object. After two drenched hours in the driving rain he was as good as gold, behaving as he knew I expected him to. General learned a lesson and so did I.

The reason horses (and kids) embarrass us with unexpected behavior is a lack of consistency on our part.

I'm a fanatic about giving precise cues and requiring precise responses from our horses at home. I expect the same response everywhere, no matter what. Teach a horse the right way to do things, be consistent, and he'll consistently do things the right way.[42] Perfection doesn't exist, but bumps in the road will be minor and easily managed.

The root cause of inconsistent teaching, whether instructing a horse or child, is either inability or unwillingness on the part of the trainer or the parent. If unable, I encourage him or her to seek instruction or get help to become able. If unwilling, that's the end of the road because someone just doesn't care enough to do the work.

The difference between great parents and others is the degree of commitment they bring to the relationship. The difference between great horse owners with successful horses and others is the level of commitment they bring to the relationship.

Consistent horses have consistent leadership.

The difference between fearless Christians and those walking around in doubt, error, and insecurity is the commitment they bring to their relationship with Jesus Christ. God doesn't change. He's the penultimate example of consistency. His rules and expectations apply in every time, in every circumstance, and to everyone.

There aren't two sets of rules for you, for kids, or for horses.

---

[42] Proverbs 22:6

Lynn Baber

Patience

"To lose patience is to lose the battle."

Mahatma Gandhi

After nine-years away from us, Shiner returned with panic attacks. Ace, his younger brother by seven days, returned with dissociative disorder. These were BIG issues that didn't resolved the first year, the second, or the third. Shiner came around sooner than Ace, but by the eighth year, Ace and Shiner were different horses. Their scars remain but are buried under new layers of lustrous, healthy personality, habit, and faith.

Two things saved Shiner and Ace; love and patience.

Horses and children are seldom born with issues. They're created by people. Sometimes you accept the responsibility to clean up the mess, committing to build something positive, productive, and beautiful. That's how you save horses.

There's no substitute for patience.

From what I hear, there are two prayers new parents pray daily when they bring their newborns home from the hospital; prayers for uninterrupted sleep and endless patience.[43] Horses entering training are like newborns; unspoiled and without vocabulary, and always assuming

---

[43] Romans 12:12, Galatians 6:9

they'll get their own way. No sane person would consider punishing a baby into some desired behavior, so why punish a horse?

If your horse isn't giving you the right answer after several attempts, come up with a new way to ask or teach. Some days I'm pressed for time with the horses, with a limited window to interact, exercise, or visit. The last thing I do is introduce something new. Little bits of time offer the perfect opportunity to share secrets, braid tails, or deep-breathe in the scent of your horse's muzzle. Create moments you can't wait to repeat. Leave your horse hoping you show up a little earlier tomorrow.

It's nearly impossible to learn something new when you're nervous, afraid, or distracted by a shiny object or sinister form lurking in the corner. Horses experience the same emotions and distractions you do. Notice your horse's energy, attention, and spirit. Oh, and one more thing, did you know that horses have hormones?

"Impatience is when your brain has a runaway to the land of fear, resistance and frustration, and drags your horse along. Horses reflect these feelings so quickly that we think it was them in the first place. Now who's confused? Magic happens when you take time to get on the same wavelength as your horse. If you're emotional, he'll be emotional. That's the wrong tune. Create places of quiet agreement and common purpose. Don't ask your horse to learn if he's nervous, afraid, or distracted."

Anna Blake, *AnnaBlakeBlog*

I wrote the paragraph prior to the quote long before I discovered the quote. When I placed it in this chapter, I noticed something odd, that Anna and I chose the same three words; *nervous, afraid,* and *distracted.* The same three words in the same order about the same thing; learning.

248

Truth is truth and horses are horses. You should find repetitive concepts between horse professionals. When you find patterns, pay extra attention.

Love is patient and kind.[44] If you're not in this for love of the horse, why are you here? God's commitment is limitless. Still, you won't be perfected this side of heaven. The work continues and requires patience (perseverance.)

———

"Patience is not indifference; patience conveys the idea of an immensely strong rock withstanding all onslaughts."

Oswald Chambers

———

[44] 1 Corinthians 13:4, Ecclesiastes 7:8, 2 Peter 3:9

Maintenance

Strangely enough, one of the easiest gaits to ride is the full-on gallop because the horse moves flat and forward. All you have to do is look ahead, stay in the middle, and smile. Whether you lope, canter, or gallop, control is a big issue. The faster a horse moves the faster his brain works. Taking delight in a morning gallop at warp speed over meadows adorned with dew drops depends on maintaining control. Flying ponytails and manes are wonderful as long as the wind tunnel is one you planned.

Teaching a horse to canter is like any other skill:

- First you have to get it.

- Then get it consistently.

- Then refine it.

Getting your horse to pick up a particular lead is NOT the same as knowing his leads. Departure, frame, cadence, and maneuverability are part of the canter experience.

Canter departures range from a simple change of footfall to precise cadenced transitions. Most horses will go faster if you encourage them, but that doesn't mean they'll go at the exact speed you have in mind, being properly balanced and prepared for precise changes in direction. Most horses never learn the nuances of canter departures yet still bless their owners with wonderful relationship and service. It's no more important in an equine soul mate than the perfect waltz is with your human soul mate.

Before asking your horse to run, be certain you can get him to stop and turn. Events happen quickly at faster gaits. You cover more ground in less time. If there's an unexpected fence or ditch ahead, you must be able to turn your horse without pulling him off balance. Horses fall down when riders pull their heads around without giving them time to re-balance their bodies. The faster you ride, the less time your horse has to compensate.

My horse Journey picks up both leads, but doesn't understand yet that left and right leads are actually a THING. We're still in the phase of getting the correct lead based on our line of travel. What I won't accept is a trot when I ask for a lope. What you teach must be maintained or it disappears. Skills and fitness levels aren't static. If you haven't used your high school French in thirty years, how fluent are you today?

I had killer legs when I was a figure skater. Five days a week I hit the ice at 4AM to work on school figures (which tells you how old I am.) The time I spent in skates equaled or exceeded the time I slept. When an orthopedic surgeon fixed what broke my skating aspirations ended. When another surgeon tried to repair my knees in 1980, I lost my killer legs because I couldn't maintain them.

But the memory is sweet.

Unlike Journey, Bo knows his leads cold. Refinement is the process of consistently schooling correct departures, frame, cadence, and maneuverability until they're automatic and precise. Horses don't stay refined unless you maintain precise responses.

Learning comes first.

Maintenance is forever.

Doubt

"Our doubts are traitors and make us lose the good we oft might win, by fearing to attempt."

William Shakespeare

Unexpected winter storms closed shop here most of one week in January. Bible studies were cancelled, the internet moved at the speed of a garden slug, and the horses seldom strayed out of the barn to investigate the outdoors. It was a week with no rehab, no riding, and little quality time together.

Am I a wimp? Surrendering to advancing age? Wait. I know there's a lesson here somewhere. It's easy to feel like I fail my horses. They're alone—without me—less than fifty feet from my office chair. Living in a barn has many perks but extreme weather still intrudes. Our horses aren't alone. Far from it. We show up multiple times a day to feed, clean, and move them in or out of their stalls. They live in a herd, so no one is ever alone unless he craves solitary meditation.

Ice dams in the gutters (I hope) left puddles in several of our bedded stalls, something I've never dealt with before. Neither have my horses. Guilt offered itself as an emotional temptation. *How can you let your little darlins have wet houses?*

Guilt happens. Very seldom, but it does.[45]

Fretting reflects an ungrateful spirit. Guilt has its place, but not in my barn. The horses are fine; only getting wet when they want to, which is far more often than I want them to. Two of my horses, Bo and Shiner, wade into standing pools of frigid water and play like toddlers, using the soles of their hooves to splash everything within ten feet with cold runny mud—including any herd mate silly enough to get within reach.

This week of objectively rotten weather, accessorized with rain and sleet, is a blessing in disguise. The horses haven't been in the pasture for two months because of drought. The pasture is crewcut short and arid silty soil doesn't hold grass roots, easily uprooted by horses walking by. In a few weeks, this spell of inconvenience will provide fresh green nibbles for the boys. Nature will breathe easier and so will we.

Like postal carriers, I'll keep delivering feed, fresh water, intermittent hug fests, and the opportunity for my guys to stretch their legs. The horses are fine because they know I'm faithful, keeping every promise. We'll live through this together, like we have everything else.

Trust

A few months after Journey arrived, I told the Lord I didn't want to walk out the rest of what Journey needed. He was broken and dangerous. I was old and unsound. I was scared, something I thought couldn't happen anymore.

---

[45] Romans 8:1, James 4:7, Romans 5:1

"Lord, I know what to do, but I don't want to."

God-engineered challenges are opportunities in disguise. Blessings. He didn't let me off the hook. I had a choice, quitting was an option, but not if I wanted God to smile. He wouldn't abandon me, but I couldn't stand knowing how much I disappointed Him.[46]

Horses learning to manage obstacles often refuse when the challenge scares them. They don't believe they can get across, over, or through it. Remember the first time you introduced your horse to a dreaded flappy plastic tarp, writhing in the breeze, making crackling noises when sand scattered on the edges?

"I can't walk on that! It's too dangerous."

"Sure you can. Let me help you with that."

Things worked out with Journey because I learned how to face fear, something I thought I was over, which is why Journey came into my life when he did. I wasn't afraid of anything. How could I be? I am a child of God; shouldn't I be fearless?

Journey brought the lesson and the blessing. I thought my doubts were about myself. My doubts weren't as much about me as about God. He proved Himself faithful. Horses also refuse to attempt scary things when they doubt the faithfulness of their rider.

"Will you take care of me? Are you sure we can do this?" Sometimes you ask the same question. Sometimes the question comes from your horse. Fear is powerful. It's

---

[46] Hebrews 13:5, Job 13:15

a biggie – the biggest biggie.

My horses are never alone. They can't always see me, but I can (almost) always see them. They'll never have to fend for themselves.

"For so many years I lived in constant terror of myself. Doubt had married my fear and moved into my mind, where it built castles and ruled kingdoms and reigned over me, bowing my will to its whispers until I was little more than an acquiescing peon, too terrified to disobey, too terrified to disagree. I had been shackled, a prisoner in my own mind.

But finally, finally, I have learned to break free."

Tahereh Mafi, *Ignite Me*

Emotion

Ellie, an intelligent nine-year-old student sat solidly in the saddle on Bailey, my handsome black Welsh lesson pony. He was his usual adorable self, the perfect gentleman, yet Ellie was bawling.

"Why are you crying?"

Sobs. Loud sucky wet ones intended to attract attention. Ellie's mother watched from the gate. She obviously thought this was my problem and watched without comment.

"Are you okay, Ellie? Why you're crying?"

More sobs.

"Are you afraid?"

Ellie nodded and kept crying.

"What are you afraid of?"

Bailey stood like a statue.

No answer from Ellie.

"Ellie, stop crying. Are you afraid of Bailey?"

Another nod and a loud sniffle. More sobs.

This was not Ellie and Bailey's first meeting. My students, regardless of age, have to fetch their steed, lead it to the grooming rack, curry and brush, clean feet, and put on the saddle. The only thing I do myself is put on the bridle.

"Did Bailey do something wrong?"

No response.

"Ellie, did Bailey do something wrong?"

She shook her head slightly, indicating "no."

"Ellie, you have no reason to be afraid of Bailey. If you want to cry, go ahead, but you can get off and your lesson is over."

That did it. Ellie stopped crying. Whatever she was trying to do didn't work. I don't babysit kids and I don't respond well to emotion divorced from reality. The lesson proceeded and Ellie made progress. Inappropriate emotions stop progress, prove authority false, and cause insecurity. They certainly cause discomfort to those watching the show. Emotions are usually self-indulgent.

Can you think of an instance where emotionalism ever produced a good result? Responding to your horses isn't as simple as "Do what I ask, or I'll work you into a frothy sweaty mess." That doesn't mean it's never wrong to drill a horse to make a point.

There are two reasons to use work as a teaching tool;

1. To expend his energy in a physical, rather than emotional way, or

2. To get the horse to focus more on your request than his own opinion of what he should be doing.

There's a big difference in the two. If a horse is already

emotional, don't pick a fight. If a horse is using its energy to resist you, give it something more useful to do with that energy. Using discipline or punishment to "correct" a fearful horse is always wrong. You can't make the right thing easy without knowing what the right thing is. There's a difference between working to gain focus and working on circles. You can't work on circles if the horse is emotionally absent.

Emotion is like an avalanche; once it careens downhill, there's no way to stop it. Your goal is to prevent avalanches from happening.

Leadership Failure

Elevated emotions don't belong in the barn.

Leadership failure is usually visible and observable if you know what to look for. Negative emotions are symptoms of leadership failure. In people, they're often indulgent, designed to attract attention like Ellie or to manipulate a situation. Whether the relationship in question is between two humans or a human and horse, there are three basic signs of leadership failure:

1. Anger

2. Anxiety

3. Aggression

Emotions are barometers of balance. Excessive emotion of any kind suggests imbalance in something; body, soul, or spirit. Anger, anxiety, and aggression begin with the same emotion – fear. The evidence of faith is peace, contentment, serenity, and hope.[47]

Aggression is a sign of leadership failure that allows an imbalance to go unnoticed or uncorrected. It's your fault when your horse reacts aggressively. You're still the bad guy when you behave aggressively toward your horse. Assertive is good. Aggression is a sign of weakness.

Horses grow stronger and bolder in right relationship with a worthy leader. Faith cannot co-exist with imbalance. Seek balance in your own life and extend the blessing to your horse. If you're emotional, out of balance, weak, or indecisive, you'll be hard-pressed to keep the promises you make your horse.

The good news, once again, is that horses are masters of forgiveness. Leadership promises freedom from anger, aggression, and anxiety. If you or your horse gets emotional, it's your responsibility to return everyone back to a calm peaceful state.

---

[47] Galatians 5:22, 1 John 4:18

Choosing a Trainer

"Trust the still, small voice that says, 'This might work, and I'll try it.'"

Diane Mariechild

Trainers are crosses between instructors, matchmakers, and therapists. Select one who understands and supports what you want, what you don't, and has the resources to help you find the right partner and do pre- and early engagement counseling. If you've already made the relationship commitment, trainers can prevent painful and costly break-ups.

Horse trainers are like physicians, either specialists or generalists. Which is the right one for you depends on your dreams, your goals, and your needs. Are you an accomplished rider but unable to start your horse from scratch, or do you need help to know which end of the horse needs the most care? Let's be honest, if there's a horse involved, either one is a fabulous place to be.

What's your goal, and what do you need to reach it you that don't already have? If you can't answer that question, spend more time taking lessons or visiting with friends and professionals. What's your dream?

Horses are expensive, eating up time, energy, and cash. Professionals exist to help you identify a doable dream and pursue it. Aside from one obvious difference, relationship with a horse is often deeper than the one shared by spouses. Don't marry one that needs to be saved, or changed, or paroled.

261

Basic Requirements of Trainers

- Love of all things about horses.
- Safety first.
- Require helmets for youth or greenhorns.
- Require a written release that makes sense.
- Offer a clean and inviting property.
- Present simple written details of costs and expectations.
- Teach care of horses not just using horses.
- Interest in your welfare and the horse's in equal measure.
- Require the physically able to groom and tack up their own mounts.
- Discuss feed programs and hoof care.
- Good communication skills that suit you.
- Share your philosophy of horses; are they tools or magical creatures?
- Consistently clean barn, clean bathroom, clean water, clean horses.
- Horses who offer themselves to visitors; inquisitive not resigned.
- Safe facilities and fencing.
- Ask in-depth questions about your experience and goals.

The saddest stories I hear as a horse trainer are about kids whose introduction to horses produced fear instead of joy because they started lessons with the wrong trainer and wrecked. Or, they jumped on a friend's horse and wrecked.

Ruining the love of horses is costly; it takes away future homes for horses who need them. It kills the dreams and passions of kids and newbies who only wanted to connect to a personal love God set in place. It's an opportunity squandered that didn't have to turn out the way it did.

Medical malpractice is seldom intentional, but the result of a doctor practicing something he or she hasn't mastered or won't commit to. Whether there wasn't enough consideration given to the situation or a lack of knowledge, the result is the same; injury or even death. Horse malpractice isn't intentional, but a similar result of a lack of concern or limited knowledge. Either way, the result is the same. Fear, injury, or worse.

Questions for prospective trainers:

- What do they feed? Hay is important: twice a day is preferable, once a day is essential.
- What is his or her philosophy of discipline?
- When something goes wrong, who gets the blame?
- How long do clients usually stick around?
- Is the horse to human ratio reasonable? No trainer can ride ten horses a day well if she has to tack, groom, clean, maintain, and feed.
- Is there daily turnout?
- What's the weekend schedule?
- Does anything change if the trainer is away competing or judging?

Certified Trainers

Should you hold out for a certified trainer? Like most

horse questions, the answer is, "it depends." I'm certified in several equine areas of expertise, but not as a trainer. When a certified trainer asked why I'm not certified I answered, "No one ever asked me. They bring me their horses because I create transformation. They get the results they want; improved relationship and better skills."

Are there certified trainers in your area? Certification alone isn't a predictor of success, but it's a good start.

You can't train a trainer. I've tried. Nothing's more difficult than sending a horse to a trainer and then trying to micro-manage her, because no one wins. Select the trainer that's best for you and your horse, who understands and appreciates your dream, and get started. If you hit a rough spot, talk it out. If differences can't be worked out without ruffled feathers, move on.

Randi Thompson, proprietor of the Ladies Horse Society, clinician, expert witness, and serial equine entrepreneur, offers these suggestions to women looking for a horse trainer or riding instructor:

- If you don't like the instructor after two or three months, switch. This is your personal journey. There's a magic that happens between women and horses. Find someone who can inspire you and make the magic live.

- Safety is always first consideration. If it's not, leave.

- Have fun!

- Choose an instructor who inspires you.

- Choose an instructor who matches or complements your personality.

- Pick a trainer as close to home as possible.

There's no need for barn drama. Sadly, it's more prevalent than not. The social and spiritual climate of a barn reflects the personality and/or limitations of the trainer or barn manager. I never allow drama in horses, clients, students, lessons, or among barn folks. The spirit of the barn is my responsibility and reflects the soul rest possible for everyone by emphasizing simple gospel principles.

Practice the golden rule, "Therefore, whatever you want men to do to you, do also to them."

Matthew 7:12

Lynn Baber

Hoofbeats on My Heart

"You took me to adventure and to love. We two have shared great joy and great sorrow. And now I stand at the gate of the paddock watching you run in an ecstasy of freedom, knowing you will return to stand quietly, loyally, beside me."

Pam Brown

Nothing is as magical as quiet time in the barn; just me, the horses, and the one Who created us. There's no angst, envy, or pressure, only perfect peace among those I love and who love me in return.[48]

Texas weather changes abruptly. In a matter of moments, the brilliant sunny skies of a balmy late-autumn day switched to ice-clouds racing across a drab gray sky as temperatures plummeted and deep frigid-winter returned. Through my office window I saw horses running for the barn, driven by the cold wind.

I went out.

The horses watched with anticipation while I fluffed mattresses with fresh shavings, brushed summer dust off winter blankets, and piled sweet-smelling flakes of luscious green hay into stall feeders. Warm waves of gratitude washed over me while I made preparation for my horses's comfort. My equine children would not be

---

[48] John 14:27

cold, hungry, or abandoned to changes in circumstance. They know me and the rhythm of my heartbeat.

With uncanny patience, the horses waited turns to come in their gates, no bustling or competing for who would be first, no backed ears or threats of a kick, just simple expectant delight in what waited within. Once each was tucked into his warm stall and pony pajamas, I closed the barn doors against the howling wind, and delighted as my horses settled into homey bliss, nurdling feed and puff-snuffling hay.

Another sunset in the barn. Blessing. Contentment. Joy.

Jesus provides what we need when we need it, regardless of changed circumstances. That's love. It's how we feel about horses and why we show up to feed and muck in the cold, the heat, the wind, the wet, and the frozen.

There is no end. There is no yesterday or tomorrow, there is only today. What you do today may be the last thing you ever do. Always leave stronger, more peaceful, richer, and more in love. In the barn and everywhere.

Fewer Horsemen

"I loved being a farm manager. I loved being a horseman. I still work the sales, even now having finished my doctorate and being considered "above" the job of yearling showman. But I love reading those young horses too much. Getting into their brains and unlocking the chains. Figuring out how to make them walk better, stand better, behave better. For a true horseman, it's an addiction; an addiction that's impossible to break. This article speaks to my equine-adoring heart and years invested, learning to be a horseman (woman.) The bustle and immediacy of our

technical world discounts the wonder, beauty, and heroism of those who love to serve and literally invest blood, sweat, and tears to learn a little more—and sometimes save a life."

Carleigh Fedorka,

Where Have All The Horsemen Gone?

I am blessed to claim much in Carleigh's article for myself. From teaching young stallions to breed, knowing what the flick of an ear means in a particular mare's cycle, to welcoming a foal's golden-slippered front feet and what follows into the world. Some of you know the feeling of reverent accomplishment from leading a panicked, broken horse back to useful, hopeful, eager relationship. But there are fewer of us. I'm not one of the greats and never will be, but I've tried and failed to find someone dedicated enough to pass along what knowledge I have.

Because it's a commitment of years. Few people want to put in the time to learn horses the way horses deserve to be known. It's no one's fault, life with horses doesn't pay in ways Warren Buffett might appreciate. There are different kinds of wealth, but fewer that the world and worldly endorse.

Life is too fast, too small, and too electronic to leave big enough spaces for a thousand-pound commitment, much less a barn full. God is good and I am grateful for the gift of decades spent in the company of horses. I know the life because I was fortunate enough to live it. And now it's passing away and we are all the poorer for it. Yet the beauty remains. It's still there.

If you have a horse, there's still time for you to drink more deeply from the chalice of all that is equine.

Why have I spent every day for decades studying,

practicing, loving, laughing, and crying over horses? Because I'll never master all that is horse.

Immovable Standards and Unlimited Grace

You need both, limitless love and concrete boundaries. Make sure the boundaries benefit your horse.

Every horse is ordinary unless made extraordinary by the woman God provides. There is no amazing horse woman without an amazing horse willing to partner with her because she proved committed, trustworthy, able, selfless in relationship, and loves the process.

Maybe the horse you have today isn't your forever horse, but every minute you spend together teaches you how to be ready once that horse shows up. Get today's lessons wrong and tomorrow's won't magically come together. The beauty of life with horses is the precious, inviting, addictive, and fulfilling effect it has on your quality of life.

Life without horses? Unimaginable. One day I'll take my last ride; maybe live in a high rise instead of a barn and won't have morning and evening chores. But the memories I'll treasure will keep my soul warm between visits from the miniature horse lady who shares her love for horses with the elderly every other Thursday.[49]

I'll sit with the others, taking turns nuzzling the soft muzzle of the generous little mini, a secret smile only visible to those who know me well. My time with horses won't be over because waiting for me beyond the narrow

---

[49] Matthew 6:2

gate to heaven50 are horses who know me better than I know myself.

Will our reunion be spectacular or what I expect; ears up, eyes fixed on my face the moment I appear? Waiting for me.

Expectant.

Glorious.

Eternal.

Blessed.

---

[50] Matthew 7:13-14

Lynn Baber

Epilogue:

Miracle Relationships

Animals see the real you. They read your spirit, your intentions, and know your heart. As a child I trusted animals and sought their company. Growing up, I took a stake in the heart on the few occasions an animal didn't immediately fall in love with me. Critters were my safe place, my comfort zone, my friends, my family.

Rejection from a person was understandable. From an animal it was traumatic. Who else is as open and tolerant? Who else loves awkward little girls without condition?

Jesus.

Relationship with horses leads to a deeper understanding and appreciation of what Jesus did for me. Unless you commit without limitations, it's impossible to grasp the magnitude of Jesus's act of love on the Cross.

"I will never leave you nor forsake you."

Hebrews 13:5

I've made that promise to quite a few horses over the years, but not all. I meant it and kept it. Sometimes the cost was significant. God, in His generous wisdom, helped me grasp the magnitude of His promises. I've never had to lay down my life for a horse or dog, but I've put it on the line more than once.

Commitment means no matter what.

273

There is no substitute for Jesus Christ, and it is not possible to be in a transformative relationship with a horse unless you are willing to be changed yourself.

We are daily called to become more like Christ. That means putting others first.

We're required to understand the unbreakable link between authority and humility. The more you learn how to be in right relationship with a horse, the deeper your understanding of Jesus becomes. I become a worthy master by submitting to the most worthy Master.

The promises of Christ become real, relevant, and as good as done.

Stewardship

Ask any horse or dog to describe the greatest gift and you'll get the same answer; a forever home and the love of someone special. But that's not always possible. Trainers welcome horses into their barns and send them home. Lives, health, and financial circumstances change. Whether your horse stays with you its entire life or one day moves on, you're still required to be a good steward.[51]

Every horse should benefit from the time it spends in your care. Stewardship does not prefer any particular philosophy of training or horse-keeping. Good stewardship doesn't demand horse shoes or snaffle bits, or endorse one feeding program over another. Good stewardship doesn't specify box stall or pasture accommodations.

---

[51] 1 Corinthians 4:2, Matthew 25:21

What it requires is attention to the health, emotional state, and needs born into every equine spirit.

Horses and Gospel Principles

The fruit of using gospel principles in relationship with a horse produces a spiritual longing in other folks for the relationship with their horse that you have with yours. Humans crave what Christ offers, but there's only one way to receive it. Other equestrians want a horse that reads their body language, offers obedience without thought, and exemplifies the miracle that is oneness with a horse. That's what relationship with Jesus is. Obedience without thought and a miraculous oneness of spirit.

Few are willing to do what is required to build such relationship. It's not the work of a day, week, or year. It's the commitment of forever, no matter how long forever turns out to be.

Once you've tasted it, there's no turning back.

"All horses deserve, at least once in their lives, to be loved by a little girl."

Unknown

Be that little girl.

Lynn Baber

About the Author

Lynn Baber is a best-selling author, World and National Champion horse trainer and breeder, former business consultant, motivational speaker, and serial entrepreneur.

Following seven years in ministry, Lynn offers clarity, simplicity, insight, and support to Christians in a post-Christian world.

Lynn also teaches horse owners how to build amazing relationship with their horses by transforming complexity into simple choices.

Lynn and her husband Baber (Larry) share the barn in Weatherford, Texas, with their horses, dogs, and cats.

Connect with Lynn at www.LynnBaber.com

Learn about the women who shared their dreams in *The Breath of Horse Crazy* from their personal pages on LynnBaber.com.

Lynn Baber

Books by Lynn Baber

GOSPEL HORSE SERIES

Book 1 – Amazing Grays, Amazing Grace

Book 2 – He Came Looking for Me

Book 3 – Discipleship with Horses

Book 4 – The Breath of Horse Crazy

HELP IN A POST-CHRISTIAN WORLD

Rapture and Revelation

Fifteen Minutes into Eternity

OTHER TITLES

The Art of Getting to YES

Christian Character

No Matter What, REJOICE!

CPSIA information can be obtained
at www.ICGtesting.com
Printed in the USA
LVHW041416170120
643849LV00002B/28